THE
MARITIME
NORTHWEST
GARDEN GUIDE

Planning Calendar for Year-Round Organic Gardening

Produced by Seattle Tilth

Table of Contents

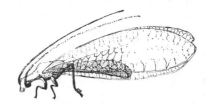

Dear Readers,

The Seattle Tilth and regional Tilth associations have served as community resources where gardeners can exchange ideas for more than 20 years. This guide is one fruit of that exchange. Tending a garden is fundamentally creating a place, a paradise specific to a region. The efforts of all the people involved in Tilth through the years focus on ways to create the paradise that is specific to our place here in the Maritime Northwest. All gardeners who have been involved with Tilth deserve the thanks for the information in this guide.

Many gardeners need a written reminder of what to do in the garden, and this guide provides a monthly checklist of gardening activities to take full advantage of our year-round gardening climate. In this new edition we have added timely and useful information to make the guide a quick resource to improve your garden and answer the most common gardening questions. Also, we hope to expand your gardening horizons by offering new suggestions.

Seattle Tilth has not invented the cultural techniques explained in this guide, but seeks to distill the experience of our community informed both by ancient tradition and more modern research and innovation. The purpose of the guide is to give gardeners the tools and skills to become their own authorities. We hope we have provided enough resources and stimulated enough ideas for you to create or expand upon your own garden paradise.

Organically,

Carl Elliott
Seattle Tilth Garden Coordinator, 1992–1998

Icons Used in This Guide

Soil Fertility:
Articles relating to building soil, composting and soil fertility.

Tilthy Tip :
Gardening secrets and tried-and-true techniques for creating a healthy garden.

Beneficial Insect:
Information on how to encourage and recognize beneficial insects.

Organic Action:
How to support organics outside the garden.

Disease Prevention:
Material related to recognizing and preventing plant diseases.

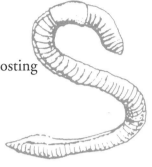

Children's Gardening:
Ideas for gardening with children at home and in school.

A Note on Varieties

Why are individual vegetable varieties so important? Plants share with other living organisms the ability to express numerous characteristics within their gene pool in response to their environment. Plants are organisms that are constantly evolving and changing. Human beings have cared for plants and selected plants that express the characteristics we desire. Taking carrots as an example, we have one variety that grows quickly in spring and another variety that does better at holding in the ground during winter. Choosing varieties suited to the season is the gardener's first criterion.

The second criterion is to choose varieties adapted to the Maritime Northwest climate. The seed business is constantly changing. Fifteen or twenty years ago it was hard to find regionally tested and adapted varieties of vegetables, or much diversity of crops listed in seed catalogs. For Maritime Northwest gardeners that is no longer the case, and we can thank our regional seed houses for their commitment to bringing gardeners high quality seeds.

The varieties of vegetables recommended in this guide have been tested at the gardens of Seattle Tilth, in the gardens of Seattle Tilth members or in P-Patches by community gardeners throughout the Northwest. Though we have tried to make the list comprehensive, seed houses are releasing new varieties all the time and rediscovering heirloom varieties. These new offerings may be improvements or they may not. We hope this guide will give you tools to find the varieties of vegetables best suited to your garden.

A Note on Botanical Names

The use of botanical Latin within this guide may seem confusing or excessive to backyard gardeners, but this was not our intention. Flowering plant families have traditionally been classified by their reproductive characteristics (flower and fruit), and this classification is useful to scientists, horticulturists and gardeners. For gardeners, knowing a bit of botanical Latin, especially plant families, makes crop rotation much easier. And when purchasing seeds or plants, gardeners will be more sure about what they are buying if they know the botanical name. Here is an example:

Bee Balm *Monarda* spp.: *M. menthifolia, M. citriodora, M. didyma*

Bee Balm is one common name for this herb; the first italicized name, *Monarda,* is the genus name describing numerous like-flowered plants; the second names (after the abbreviated genus name, *M.*) are the individual species (spp.) names; *menthifolia:* mint-like leaves; *citriodora*: lemon-scented; and *didyma*: leaves in pairs. All three are species within the genus *Monarda*.

What is Organic Gardening?

...Well, it isn't rocket science—organic gardening is a lot more complex. Rocket science seeks to accomplish something unnatural by isolating and controlling all relevant factors. Organic gardening seeks a delicate balance between leaving nature alone and manipulating it to produce crops. Organic gardening practices should nurture and enhance life in a diverse and complex ecosystem, and ensure the long-term ability of the soil to produce crops. The following principles, developed throughout this guide, are a starting point for helping you to become a beneficial organism in your garden.

Care For the Soil

The few of us who live on top of the soil are deeply indebted to the many working within it. A gram of healthy soil is home to as many as 500 million beings—bacteria, actinomycetes, fungi, yeasts, protozoa, algae, etc. Soil organisms create and maintain a complex warehouse and distribution system capable of storing and moving an abundant yet balanced supply of essential nutrients. The gardener's most important job is to protect and help these creatures by composting; planting cover crops; adding organic soil amendments; paying attention to soil, air and water contents; and learning other beneficial practices.

Practice Crop Rotation

Rotating crops is the practice of not planting the same kind of plant in the same place year after year. Rotation is important both for soil care and pest reduction. The soil nutrient distribution system constantly makes nutrients available to plants, but at a slow rate. Different plants use different nutrients at different rates. If you grow corn every year in the same spot, you will use up corn's most important nutrients at a faster rate than the soil can provide them. If you wait a long time between each planting of corn, the soil has the chance to build up its store of corn nutrients. A useful rotation is leaf to root to flower to fruit. For example, grow a leafy plant such as cabbage in the spring, a root crop such as beets in the fall, a flowering cover crop or cut flowers and finally a fruit crop such as cucumbers in the summer.

Many pests depend upon a specific host plant family (for example, the cabbage maggot needs to eat broccoli, cauliflower, turnips or other members of the cabbage family). Rotation is a way to move plant families around to disrupt and confuse the pests. If you grow broccoli in Bed A this year, grow it in Bed B next year, and plant non-cabbage-family members in Bed A for three to five years.

Encourage Diversity

It is exciting to learn about the many complex interactions that take place in a garden ecosystem— who is eating whom, what effects does a given plant or animal have on its environment? We will never, however, be able to perceive, understand or control all that is going on. A prudent approach is to assume that, generally, more diversity is better. Try to grow the greatest variety of plants that you can—tall, short, perennial, annual, deep- or shallow-rooted, flowering in different months, different colors, seedy, fruity, rooty, live, dead, etc. Each will provide habitat and food for different creatures. You don't need to know what they are all doing to appreciate the results of their work.

Pay Attention

In the garden we humans are big, lumbering, dull creatures often oblivious to most of the interactions going on about us. It is important to use the senses we have to their fullest. Not only will paying attention help us make better decisions in influencing our garden ecosystem, but learning and gaining confidence from our own observations can be as rewarding as better vegetable flavor. Your own observations can tell you more than volumes of gardening books. For example, should you do something to decrease the aphids in your garden, or is there enough evidence of parasitic wasps and lady beetles to suggest that you just leave the aphids alone?

Read On

While your own observations are your best learning tool, you don't have to learn everything all by yourself. Observations about how and when to grow crops best are part of local and regional culture. This guide provides information for beginners to get a jump on learning about growing crops in the Maritime Northwest, and serves as a reference for experienced gardeners.

The Maritime Northwest's climate makes it possible to garden here year round. By using the right varieties, planting at the right time and using even the simplest season extenders, it's surprising how much can be grown through even our harshest winters. Although our mild climate provides the potential for year-round gardening, several strategies must be employed to realize this potential. Here are four basic strategies:

Strategies for Year-Round Gardening

Use Varieties Suited to the Seasons

Many crops can be grown year round; in most cases different varieties are best adapted to different seasons. The best seed catalogs provide such information, identifying, for example, summer and winter lettuces. Seed companies that focus on cooler northern climates or our particular Maritime Northwest climate are most useful in this regard. Use the many seasonal variety suggestions in this book, or try others. By experimenting with new varieties and noting successes or failures, you can learn which crops do best in your situation. See page 11 for a list of seed sources.

Extend the Growing Season

Season extenders lengthen the effective growing season by creating protected environments under cover. Used in early spring, propagation boxes, cold frames, cloches and greenhouses give tender plants a head start so they will be more likely to mature during our often cool summers. For details on making and using season extenders, see *Gardening Under Cover* by William Head.

There are so many possibilities for extending the growing season that it can easily become confusing. For example, you can start parsley indoors under lights in February, in a cold frame in March or directly in the ground in April. Which is best for you? If you want a longer growing season, you have to decide which plants you want to use season extenders for and how early you want a crop.

Propagation boxes include a source of *supplemental light* and *bottom heat* to facilitate seed germination in early spring. This is especially useful for long-season crops such as leeks, celery and tomatoes. A few seed catalogs and garden stores sell propagation chambers, but you can also buy the components and make your own.

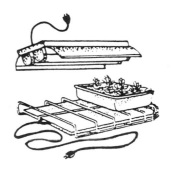

Maritime Northwest houses almost never have as much indoor light as garden starts need. Direct sunlight indoors is limited in winter by clouds and in summer by the angle of the sun. *Indirect* light loses intensity dramatically even a few inches inside the window. Plants started indoors will grow much better with supplemental light. A good technique is to hang fluorescent lights from chains or ropes so you can adjust their height. Adjust the lamp so it's 1 or 2 inches from the tops of your plants. Incandescent bulbs are too hot; if they are close enough to a plant to provide significant light, they will burn it. Use inexpensive timers to control lighting periods.

Bottom heat can greatly improve germination rates. Once the plants are up and growing, they no longer need the bottom heat (but they still need strong light). All sorts of bottom heating devices are available and, although expensive, they are worth the investment. A heating pad with a thermostat works best. Cheaper heating cables covered by moist sand also work, but are more difficult to set up. If you don't want to buy bottom heaters, any place that can provide a consistent 70° F until germination (such as the top of a radiator) will do. Be inventive.

Windowsills filled with germinating plants are a sure sign of spring. Windows with sunny southern and western exposures can be used to start seeds in March without bottom heat (assuming you heat your house). Using windowsills before March is unlikely to afford seedlings enough light. If plants are spindly and pale green they probably aren't getting enough light.

Cloches are easy-to-move protection devices usually made of (or covered with) clear plastic or glass. A typical cloche consists of a sheet of clear plastic draped over a tunnel made of plastic hoops. In the spring, plants in a cloche will grow more quickly than unprotected plants. Cloches are also used to harden off transplants (see pg. 30), and to warm garden soil before seeds are sown. As the soil dries out under a cloche it heats up, and this added warmth is critical for germinating seeds. Used in this way, cloches can extend the spring growing season by two or three weeks, or keep it "on schedule" in a particularly wet spring. Used in the fall, they provide protection from the first frosts and prolong the harvest of tender and half-hardy plants by a few weeks. They also protect overwintering vegetables from wind, rain and cold. A good cloche provides protection while remaining easy to vent and move. Its great advantages are mobility and flexibility.

Cold frames perform many of the same functions as cloches, but are more permanent structures. They are made of sturdy walls with a transparent glass, plastic or fiberglass cover that is easy to open. The opaque walls block some light, but also hold in a bit more heat. Cold frames can be particularly useful for hardening off transplants, providing protection in an especially cold spot or enhancing heat in an already warm site.

Hot beds are cold frames with a source of bottom heat. The easiest hot beds to use have a heating cable buried about 8 inches deep, which allows for very early germination. Traditional hot beds are made by burying fresh manure beneath the growing soil; the heat from the decomposing manure warms the seeds above.

Solar greenhouses not only do everything cold frames and cloches do, but they also prolong the growing season by capturing extra light and heat during the winter months. Mizuna mustard overwintered in a greenhouse, for example, will be ready to harvest at least one month earlier than mizuna overwintered under a cloche. Greenhouses are good places to start seeds in flats, and in the summer you can use them to grow heat-loving crops such as basil, eggplant, peppers and tomatoes. Greenhouses are quite expensive. Before buying or building one, consider whether it is really necessary, then study possible designs carefully.

Plant in Succession

"I can't grow cilantro; it just goes to seed." This common complaint illustrates the need to practice succession sowing. Rather than sowing a big patch of cilantro and watching it bolt (go to seed), sow a little bit each week or two from February through August. Eat each sowing of cilantro when it's young and tender.

A good candidate for succession sowing is any crop that you eat fresh, doesn't hold well in the garden or grows quickly enough to produce more than once per year. Think about how much of this vegetable you will eat in a week or two, and sow only a little more than that much seed every week or two. For example, if you eat two heads of lettuce per week, sow six seeds per week; if more than three seeds come up, either thin to three plants, or only transplant three (or two if you have no fears about slugs!). Choose varieties that are best suited to each season.

Another approach to succession planting is to take advantage of the varying lengths of time different varieties take to mature. For example, to have fresh broccoli over a several week period, sow three different varieties on the same day —seeds that mature in 60, 70, and 80 days. Sow as many seeds of each variety as you will eat in 10 days, plus some extra to make up for low germination and pest damage.

The key to successions is to plan ahead. Think about how much you want to harvest and when, and count backwards to know when to sow. Write a sowing schedule on your calendar to help you remember. Plants grow at different rates throughout the year, so you may need to sow fewer seeds more frequently for warm season harvests and more seeds less frequently for cool season harvests. Keep track of sowing and harvest dates and adjust your schedule the following year.

Make Use of Transplants

Transplanting is a way to give many types of plants a head start in early spring. Some plants, such as eggplants and peppers, can only be grown in the Maritime Northwest if sown under cover several weeks before it is warm enough to transplant them outdoors.

Using transplants is also helpful for making the best use of garden space and for timing successions. At the height of summer, for example, when it's time to sow winter vegetables, most avid gardeners don't have room to plant even a single radish. By sowing the seeds in containers or a nursery bed, the plants get a good start on growth by the time the harvest of an earlier crop makes room for them in the garden.

Transplants can also minimize the time that the soil is bare. For example, while your spring broccoli seedlings are growing inside, your garden can be growing cover crops. When it's time to transplant, you can move the cover crop to the compost pile and transplant the broccoli, which will grow more quickly than it would have if it was just starting out from seed.—RP

What is a Maritime Climate?

Gardeners rarely thank the weather. It seems there is always something to complain about: it's too cold or too hot, too wet or too dry. In the Maritime Northwest, the climate brings steady, moist and mild weather that can drive even the most casual sun worshipper to distraction.

Nonetheless, we should remember to thank the giant Pacific Ocean for providing a climate that is fairly even the whole year round. The sheer size of the ocean causes solar warmth to be slowly accumulated and slowly released, moderating the temperature changes through the seasons. The winds from the ocean bring moderately cool, moist air across the Northwest in winter and summer months. The geographic areas most affected by an onshore flow of mild marine air are said to have a maritime climate.

The topography of the Northwest also defines the maritime climate. The Cascade mountains protect and insulate the Pacific coast from inland weather patterns. Maritime Northwest weather results from the complex interactions of onshore weather and continental or inland weather. For example, the very cold weather of midwinter often flows over the Cascades or through the Columbia Gorge and meets wet clouds in the west—this often results in snow or, along the gorge, ice storms.

Our cool but moderate springs seem to last well into June, and long drawn-out cool fall weather often starts in late August and remains mild into November. This makes first and last frost dates unpredictable. Therefore, when planting out or sowing, it's more important to focus on soil temperature, which more accurately defines the growing and harvesting seasons of the Maritime Northwest. Although we may not be experiencing frost, our cool night temperatures in the spring and fall make it especially important to have adequate soil warmth for less hardy plant varieties. A soil thermometer is especially useful when the seasons are changing.

Most of the sowing dates in this guide correspond to an approximate time when the temperature and light conditions are appropriate for each crop (in the Puget Sound Basin). In developing this guide, numerous sources were queried and years of sowing information compiled from the Seattle Tilth gardens and Maritime Northwest gardeners. However, the weather can never be accurately predicted and exact sowing dates can change considerably from year to year.

To make sowing predictions a little easier, the Maritime Northwest can be divided into zones that provide more specific information about what each area can expect when onshore weather and continental or inland weather interact. Gardeners can use this information to adjust planting dates for their microclimate.

Map Key and Zone Descriptions

The letters designating different zones are only for the purposes of a map key. The map takes into consideration first and last frost dates, heat units accumulated throughout the growing season and annual rainfall. It is impossible to give perfectly accurate definitions of the zones; anyone living close to a boundary will experience attributes of both zones. Other influences can create microclimate environments within the zones that can cause variations of 5° to 7° F.

We hope these zones will help gardeners develop a better understanding of their microclimates. Seattle Tilth wishes to thank Raintree Nursery for permission to use the map, and the late Don Shakow for defining the zones and developing the map.

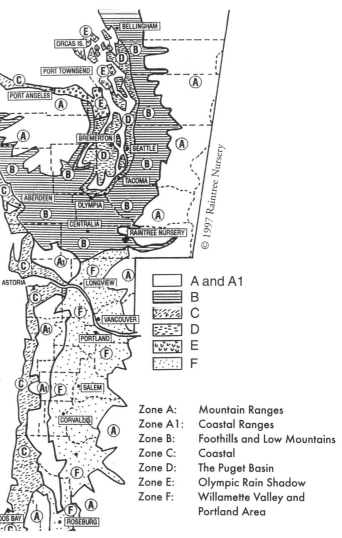

MARITIME NORTHWEST CLIMATE MAP

© 1997 Raintree Nursery

Zone A:	Mountain Ranges
Zone A1:	Coastal Ranges
Zone B:	Foothills and Low Mountains
Zone C:	Coastal
Zone D:	The Puget Basin
Zone E:	Olympic Rain Shadow
Zone F:	Willamette Valley and Portland Area

ZONE A: THE MOUNTAIN RANGES

If you are already actively vegetable gardening in this mountain area, more power to you. The truly frost-free season is nonexistent; any day of the year can bring frost, though the summers can be quite pleasant. Vegetables outside during the summer growing season need to be hardy and able to survive cold nights. Choose vegetables listed in this guide for early spring and fall sowing, but start them in May or June for harvest in September. Winter gardening is, of course, left to the resourceful.

ZONE A1: THE COASTAL RANGE

The low mountains of the coastal range experience a bit of a moderating influence from the ocean, so winters are not as cold as in the inland heights. The summers in general are cool, so typical summer fruits are difficult to grow outside without the protection of a cloche or cold frame. The more difficult peppers and eggplants probably should be left to the adventurous. When choosing vegetables, look to hardy and half-hardy varieties, saving the sub-tropical for a novelty. Winter gardening can be dicey unless you have a favorable mini-micro-climate and protect plants with mulches, cloches or cold frames.

ZONE B: FOOTHILLS AND LOW MOUNTAINS

This area experiences a blending effect of the moderating air of the Puget Sound and the ocean with a strong mountain influence. The rain clouds frequently back up against the mountains, resulting in twice as much annual rainfall as in the lowlands. Cold frost often moves through the Frasier River

Valley (in British Columbia) and other mountain valleys to cause extreme winter lows. Last frost dates are around mid-May to June, with the first frost occurring in early October. The approximate sowing dates in this guide will be most useful if you sow two to three weeks later in the spring, and two to three weeks earlier in the summer and fall. Winter minimum temperatures are often in the teens and below, so winter gardening works well if plants are given adequate protection with mulches, cloches and cold frames.

ZONE C: COASTAL

This is a weatherperson's dream climate: It's a good bet that it will be raining and in the '50s most days of the year. Winters are quite mild, with minimum temperatures generally a few degrees higher than inland areas, and in summer, fog and low heat make this area a salad green grower's paradise. Most of the sowing dates in this guide will be appropriate for the coast, although summer vegetables can be difficult to grow here due to cool summer nights. Strong winds make it important to create wind breaks or seek out a sheltered spot for your garden.

ZONE D: THE PUGET BASIN

This is a blessed microclimate kissed by the salt water winds of Puget Sound. Minimum winter temperatures vary widely depending on the proximity of your garden to the salt water. The average minimum is 15° to 20° F, though some island locales have an average low temperature 5° F higher than mainland areas. Frost pockets are common in the small valleys of this undulating landscape. Population density and pavement have created mini-microclimates throughout much of the basin, slightly raising both summer and winter temperatures. The frost-free period begins around April 15 and ends around Oct. 31. The summers can be cool and cloudy, though sunnier than coastal areas. Heat-loving summer crops must be chosen for their ability to withstand cool nights, and should be situated where they can get the most sun and warmth.

ZONE E: OLYMPIC RAIN SHADOW

Protected from heavy southern rain storms by the Olympic Mountains, the rain shadow is a crescent-shaped area that extends from Port Townsend/Port Angeles across upper Whidbey Island and the San Juan Islands to the southern tip of Vancouver Island. On average, this zone experiences warmer winter temperatures than other parts of the Puget Basin. However, very low temperatures can occur if a cold front moves in from the Frasier River Valley. Cool, foggy summers with winds blasting in from the Strait of Juan de Fuca can impede ripening of summer fruit. Tender vegetables benefit from a cloche all summer long. However, winter gardens are at their best in this region, as it has a long growing season for cool-weather plants. A good water conservation program is important because rainfall is significantly lower here than in other areas of the Maritime Northwest.

ZONE F: WILLAMETTE VALLEY AND PORTLAND AREA

This zone has complex weather variations. Due to its slightly inland location it has a greater fluctuation of temperatures from winter to summer. In general, the summers here are the warmest of the Maritime Northwest, especially around Corvallis and along the Umpqua River. Most summer fruits grow well if attention is paid to appropriate varieties. In the depths of winter, valley cold pockets regularly experience temperatures below 15° F for extended periods of time. When this is the case, overwintered vegetables need the protection of a cloche or mulch.

In hilly districts, two kinds of mini-microclimates are frequently found: frost pockets in the valleys and protected south facing slopes that warm well during the growing season. As the valleys slope up to the foothills, the severity of cold weather increases and the growing season is shortened. For this zone, estimate approximate sowing dates two weeks earlier in the spring and two weeks later in the summer and fall than indicated in this guide. This is particularly true when planting out summer fruit crops.—CE

January

In the Garden

January provides the perfect conditions for imagining and planning a garden. The foliage has died back revealing the true shape of your garden, it seems quieter with fewer plants competing for your attention, and the wide open spaces can help inspire your imagination. A stroll around the January garden is full of promise.

A well-thought-out garden plan for the year can help you resist the temptation of the seed catalog writer's florid descriptions. It helps if you maintain a balance of plants you have grown successfully in the past and new varieties you want to test out. Plant again your "bests" from last year while leaving some room for experimentation.

Today's gardening world offers myriad mail order seed companies from which to choose. The past 20 years have seen an increase in quality seed houses catering to backyard gardeners. Ordering seeds by mail may not be cheaper than buying from seed racks, but the seed is often of better quality and there is significantly more variety.

Most vegetable garden seed, when properly cared for, can maintain vigor for more than three to five years. The seed life as listed on the packet assumes the average gardener stores seeds in a shoe box in a warm house. The key to lengthening the life of seeds is to lower the relative humidity and temperature at which they are stored. Any good container with a tight fitting lid will do, such as a Tupperware tub or a five-gallon food bucket. Place a few silica gel desiccant packets among the seed packets and seal the bucket. Store the container in a cool part of the house that is not damp (or in an extra refrigerator). When sowing time comes around, bring out only those seeds you need to sow for the next few weeks.—CE

Janus

Janus was a Roman deity with two faces who presided over the threshold of endeavors. As Janus, looking forward and looking back, you can use both foresight and hindsight to plan your garden.

Good Starts: Tips for Starting Seeds

Wide variety makes it difficult to make general rules about starting seeds; however we can list a few to assist a gardener in getting off to a good start (pun intended).

🐝 Use a good potting mix or prepare a loose seed bed with good tilth. Seeds need to push up out of the soil, so large clods or heavy soil impede their imminent emergence.

🐝 In general, cover the seed with a soil depth 3 times the thickness of the seed (not the length or width, but the thickness, i.e. 3 times the diameter of round seeds; only millimeters deep for very thin seeds like those of the carrot). Heavier soil cover can work, but at first sow too many seeds and cover with a little soil; thinning is easier than re-sowing.

🐝 For small seeds (like those of the carrot), avoid sowing too many seeds and help anchor them in the soil by mixing the seeds with sand before sowing.

🐝 Make sure the soil is adequately warm. This guide will give you general planting times that take into consideration appropriate soil temperature, but nothing beats going out and testing for yourself. Try setting a soil thermometer in plant beds or under cloches to evaluate when the soil is ready to sow. A thermometer is not necessary, but can be a helpful tool. As a general rule for spring crops, a soil temperature (at seed depth) in the 50's or 60's results in fair germination. For summer crops, the soil temperature needs to be in the high 60's—this is why they are sown indoors or under cloches.

🐝 Keep the soil evenly moist until the seed leaves emerge. This can be done by watering frequently or by covering seed flats with sheets of glass or plastic to reduce evaporation. To prevent damping off diseases, it is very important to remove the covering immediately after the seed leaves emerge.

🐝 Once the seed shows its first seed leaves, water less. Let the surface of the soil dry out between watering. Very lightly stir the surface of the soil with a table fork or stick. This cultivation aerates the soil surface and reduces disease organisms that thrive in moist soil.

🐝 Seeds require higher temperatures to germinate than plants need to grow. If possible, lower the soil temperature once the seedlings have emerged (by turning off any heating devices or moving the flats to a cooler place).

🐝 Improve air circulation. For indoor plants, use a small fan to blow air across the surface of the soil; vent cloches and cold frames to ensure air flow. Lack of air circulation is the primary cause of damping-off organisms that kill seedlings.—CE

Sow Indoors

Sow indoors to transplant to the garden. Plants that need a long time before they are planted out to the garden can be grown with the aid of supplementary light and heat (see Propagation Boxes, pg. 3). Faster-growing varieties can be transplanted under a cloche.

VEGETABLES AND HERBS

ONION FAMILY *Alliaceae*
    Leeks: Varna, Otina, Splendid, Le Lyon
    Onions: Copra, Simcoe, Buffalo, Stuttgarter
SUNFLOWER FAMILY *Compositae*
    Artichoke: Imperial Star, Northern Star, Green Globe
    Cardoon
    Endive: President, Perfect
    Lettuce: Winter Density, Little Gem, Rouge d'Hiver,
        Perella, Capitaine, Rougette du Midi
ROSE FAMILY *Rosaceae*
    Alpine Strawberries

FLOWERS

Supplementary heat and light are necessary to get an early start with these slow-growing perennials and annuals. All will bloom the first year if started now.

Annuals and short lived perennials to bloom the first year
Bee Balm *Monarda* spp.: *M. menthifolia, M. citriodora, M. didyma*
Carnations and Pinks *Dianthus* spp.: Cottage Pinks, Spring
    Beauty, Rainbow Loveliness
Dahlia (from seed)
Geraniums *Pelargonium* spp.
Heliotropium arborescens
Lawn Daisy *Bellis perennis:* Habenera, White Carpet
Mallow *Malva sylvestris:* Bibor Felho, Zebrina
Petunia
Plummed Thistle *Cirsium japonicum*: Early Rose Beauty
Prairie Gentian *Eustoma grandiflorum*
Roman Chamomile *Anthemis nobilis*
Snapdragon *Antirrhinum* spp.: Rocket White, Peaches and
    Cream, Black Prince
Spurge *Euphorbia marginata*: Summer Icicle
Viola: Spring Pansies, Johnny Jump-ups, Awkright Ruby, Prince John
Wallflower *Cheiranthus cheiri, Erysimum concinnum*
Wax Begonia: Coco mixed, Excel, Viva
Wax Flower *Cerinthe major* var. *purpurascens*
Yarrow *Achillea* spp.: Summer Pastels, Colorado

Seed Houses

A sampling of seed houses recommended by Seattle Tilth:

Abundant Life Seed Foundation P.O. Box 772, Port Townsend, WA 98368; 360-385-5660; Email: abundant@olypen. Specializes in preserving rare open-pollinated seeds from the Pacific Rim. Request free information or newsletter. Catalog $2. www.csf.colorado.edu/perma/abundant

Bountiful Gardens 18001 Shafer Ranch Rd.,Willits, CA 95490-9626; 707-459-6410 Email: bountiful@zapcom.net All seeds are from Chase Organics in England, or are grown locally and biointensively in Willits. A project of Ecology Action with proceeds funding research on small-scale farming and gardening.

Companion Plants 7247 N. Coolville Ridge Rd., Athens, OH 45701; 740-592-4643; fax 740-593-3092. A superb source of herb seeds and plants. Large packets of seed with excellent germination. Free catalog.

The Cook's Garden P.O. Box 5010, Hodges, SC 29653-5010; 800-457-9703, fax 800-457-9705. Salads, salads, salads. Perpetual spinach/chard, an extensive listing of chicories, and the best mesclun (yuppie chow) mixes in the U.S.A. are just the beginning of these green delights. Free catalog. www.cooksgarden.com

Filaree Farm 182 Conconully Hwy., Okanogan, WA 98840; 509-422-6940. With more than 100 varieties, this is the widest selection of garlic in the country. Contact filaree@cascades.net to request a catalog. www.organic-growers.com/growers/USA/filaree-farm.htm.

Garden City Seeds 778 Hwy 93 N, Hamilton, MT 59840; 406-961-4837; fax 406-961-4877; Email: seeds@montana.com This catalog offers the best for both farmers and city gardeners. With most seeds organically grown, this is a resource for sustainable development and agriculture. Free catalog. www.gardencityseeds.com

Horizon Herbs P.O. Box 69, Williams, OR 97544-0069 541-846-6704; fax 541-846-6233; Email: herbseed@chatlink. Strictly medicinal herbs, with useful cultural & historical information and nice illustrations. www.chatlink.com/~herbseed

J.L. Hudson, Seedsman Box 1058, Redwood City, CA 94064-1058; no phone calls. The Ethnobotanical Catalog of Seeds is probably the most diverse collection of seed offered for sale in the country. Catalog $1.

Johnny's Selected Seeds 1 Foss Hill Road, Albion, ME 04910-9731; 207-437-4301; fax 1-800-437-4290. A very reliable seed house for the gardener; unique varieties for cool summer areas. www.johnnyseeds.com

Larner Seeds P.O. Box 407, Bolinas, CA 94924; 415-868-9407. Wildflowers for Western Landscapes is the source for many annual flowers native to the West Coast; extensive native grass offerings.Catalog $2.

Nichols Garden Nursery 1190 Old Salem Rd., Albany, OR 97321-4580; 541-928-9280; fax 1-800-231-5306. An established herb and specialty vegetable catalog with some great root crop offerings. www.nicholsgardennursery.com

Pinetree Garden Seeds P.O. Box 300, New Gloucester, ME 04260; 207-926-3400; fax 1-888-52SEEDS; pinetree@superseeds.com. Reasonably priced seed packets for the home gardener, many under $1. www.superseeds.com

Richter's Herbs 357 Hwy. 47, Goodwood, Ontario, Canada L0C 1A0; 905-640-6677; fax 905-640-6641. Culinary and medicinal herb seeds. www.richters.com

Continued on page 12

Salt Spring Seeds Box 444, Ganges P.O., Salt Spring Island, B.C., Canada, V8K 2W1; 250-537-5269. A great selection of staple grains and pulses. An enchanting array of dried beans. All seeds organically grown and open-pollinated. www.saltspring.com

Seed Savers Exchange 3076 N. Winn Rd., Decorah, IA 52101; 319-382-5990. Thousands of members from around the world exchanging more than 6,000 seeds from which a member chooses one to "adopt" by committing to grow and re-list the seed in the future. Beginners can pick a plant that they already have a fondness for, grow it, and save the seed. $25 Membership is worth every penny. www.seedsavers.org

Seeds of Change P.O. Box 15700, Santa Fe, NM 87506-5700; 888-762-7333; gardener@seedsofchange.com. 100 percent organic, open-pollinated, and non-GMO seeds & bulbs. Free general catalog. If you are an avid plant hunter, ask for the Deep Diversity Catalog by Alan Kapular, PhD, for $5. www.seedsofchange.com

Seeds Trust High Altitude Gardens P.O. Box 1048, Hailey, ID 83333-1048; 208-788-4363; fax 208-788-3452; support@seedsave.org.

Heirloom tomatoes from Siberia and beyond, and a fine wildflower collection. Good selections for short season areas. Catalog $1. www.highaltitudegardens.com

Territorial Seed Company P.O. Box 157, Cottage Grove, OR 97424-0061; 541-942-9547; fax 1-888-657-3131. The brassica selection is the best, along with peppers, tomatoes, and many others that will thrive in the Maritime Northwest. A free, must-have catalog. www.territorial-seeds.com

Thompson & Morgan Dept. 181-3, P.O. Box 1308, Jackson, NJ 08527; 1-800-274-7333; fax 1-888-466-4769; Email: tminc@thompson-morgan.com American sales from an English seed house; 3,000 varieties of flowers and vegetables, with many unobtainable elsewhere. A bit pricey for the amount of seed; but if you must have it, what can you do? www.thompson-morgan.com

West Coast Seeds Unit 206-8475 Ontario St., Vancouver, B.C. Canada V5X 3E8; 604-482-8800; fax 604-482-8822. This company emphasizes seed varieties (all non-GMOs) suitable to the Maritime Northwest. www.westcoastseeds.com

Crop Rotation Techniques

Crop rotation is often the least practiced organic cultural technique among small-scale gardeners. Good garden space is limited in a city and the temptation is high to grow your favorite crops in the same place year after year. There are two primary reasons to practice crop rotation. The first is disease and insect prevention, and the second is soil fertility management. Proper crop rotation is an easy way to prevent pests and diseases while managing adequate soil fertility.

The crop plants that are in the same plant families tend to share insects and diseases. For example, radishes and

broccoli are susceptible to root maggot (a fly larvae) and club-root (a soil-dwelling fungus that causes the malformation of brassica roots). There are many examples of overlapping problems within every plant family. Growing crops from the same plant family in the same spot year after year builds up populations of disease organisms and damaging insect populations specific to that family. This makes subsequent crops more susceptible to damage or complete failure.

As a general rule, plan to wait three to seven years between growing crops of the same family in the same

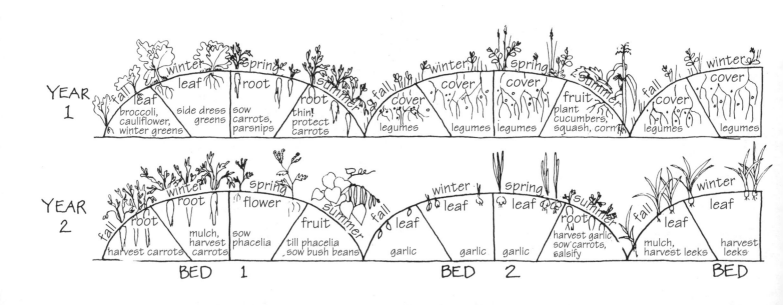

bed. This is especially important for the Nightshade family (*Solanaceae*), the Onion family (*Alliaceae*) and the Cabbage family (*Brassicaceae*). Although long-term disease and insect problems are less common among other families of cultivated plants, rotation is important for all crop plants.

This gardening guide lists crop plants alongside the names of their families to help gardeners more effectively plan crop rotations.

Another aspect of crop rotation involves maximizing soil fertility. This type of crop rotation is used on organic farms to minimize inputs of fertilizer or manures. Briefly stated, under organic culture soil nutrients are not extracted by plants at the same rate. Nitrogen tends to be used up or leached out relatively quickly after application. Phosphorus, potassium, calcium and trace minerals often remain in adequate amounts for a few seasons after being applied to a soil with good structure and organic matter. Crop rotation takes advantage of this nutrient availability. As a rotation prototype, think of a succession from leaf to root to flower to fruit. The part of the plant you harvest and consume will fit into one of these four categories.

Start off a rotation with leaf crops that are well-manured and fertilized. Most leaf crops require large amounts of nitrogen to put on good growth. These plants benefit from a rich, well-prepared bed.

After harvest, plant root crops that require less nitrogen and more potassium and trace minerals. No additional inputs of organic fertilizer are necessary, but compost could be added.

Flowers are next in the rotation to provide both nectar for beneficial insects and food for the gardener's soul. Annual flowers are frequently light feeders and require no addition of compost or organic fertilizer. At the Seattle Tilth gardens, we often sow buckwheat, phacelia or marigolds as a cover crop to bloom and be turned under if we do not want to cut flowers. Legume cover crops can be grown as the flower part of the rotation, then they can be turned under to prepare the soil for tender summer fruit crops.

The tender summer fruits such as tomatoes, peppers and corn grow well in a soil rich with nutrients and organic matter resulting from a cover crop. Many gardeners get stuck growing only summer fruits, and at best rotating with a winter cover crop. This can be done for a number of years but can eventually lead to a build-up of pest populations and disease organisms.

Instead of greedy summer fruits, small grains and pulses can be grown with no additional inputs because their nutrient needs are relatively low. Try fava beans or peas. Small grains also require comparatively low levels of nutrients for respectable yields.

Looking at soil fertility alone, the rotation could begin again with heavy-feeding leaf crops grown in a well-manured and fertilized bed.

The sample rotations in the chart below illustrate these principles. Many variations exist and can be tailored to your growing needs.—CE

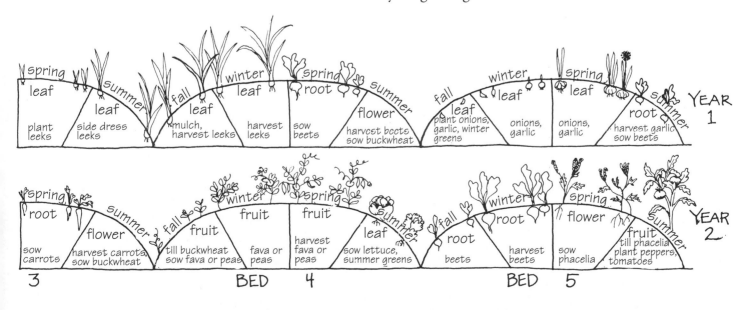

February

In the Garden

February in the Maritime Northwest brings rain, rain and more rain. What does all this water do to the soil? During this time of year our soils become saturated—all the pore space within the soil becomes filled with water. This can become a problem for the gardener because cultivating saturated soil damages its structure, doing more harm than good. A cloche built over a garden bed warms the soil and reduces the amount of rain that falls on the bed. The soil will not dry out quickly, so a cloche may need to be in place two to three weeks before the ground is ready to plant.

To test if the soil is workable, dig down 6 to 8 inches and gather a handful of soil. Gently compress the soil into a ball with one hand. Toss the ball 6 inches into the air and let it fall into your open hand. If the ball falls apart into crumbs, the soil is ready to work; if it stays as a ball or only comes slightly apart, more drying time is necessary.

Tradition in these parts is to "sow your peas by Presidents' Day." You can also sow early spring greens in late February. Sow the seeds in relatively shallow soil so they will warm during the day. Most of these plants germinate well at 50° to 60° F, the usual temperature of the top 2 inches of soil on sunny days this month. A soil or compost thermometer is useful for checking soil temperature, and can be used for other crops as the season progresses.

Perennial plants that bloom in late spring, summer and fall can be safely divided in February. The center of many older perennials turns woody and unproductive, which results in a doughnut effect of healthy plant material surrounding a dead center. Take out the whole plant and separate parts of the crown by prying it apart with two small garden forks, or cutting the crown into smaller pieces with a sharp knife or machete. Discard the old woody center and keep the outside new growth for future plants. Before replanting, renew the soil where you are going to plant by forking in compost and soil amendments.—CE

Februum

The dawn of the agricultural year was honored by medieval Anglo-Saxon farmers by placing a loaf of bread under the first furrow they plowed. Spring cleaning may have begun with Februum, a Roman ritual cleansing ceremony when lavender and other herbs were used to scent houses.

Sow Outdoors

VEGETABLES AND HERBS

Late February

Very hardy vegetables and herbs can be sown outdoors towards the end of February. A cloche is sometimes useful to warm the soil, but is not necessary. These plants can take frost down to 25° F with little damage.

CARROT FAMILY *Apiaceae*
  Chervil: Brussels Winter, Turnip-Rooted
  Fennel
  Sweet Cicely
FLAX FAMILY *Linaceae*
  Flax, Edible: Golden
MUSTARD FAMILY *Brassicaceae*
  Arugula, Rustic: *Arugula sylvatica*
  Radishes: French Breakfast, Fluo, Easter Egg, White Icicle
ONION FAMILY *Alliaceae*
  Garlic (cloves): Italian Red, California Early, Polish White, Silver Rose
  Shallots (bulbs): French Grey, Frog's Leg, French Red
  Potato Onions (bulbs)
  Onion Sets (for Green Onions)
PEA FAMILY *Fabaceae*
  Fava Beans: Aquadulce, Bonnie Lad, The Sutton, Broad Windsor, Green Windsor, Random Lilac, Mr. Barton's
  Snow Peas: Oregon Giant, Oregon Sugar Pod, Carouby de Maussane, Golden Sweet, Dwarf Grey Sugar
  Shelling Peas: Petit Pois, Waverex, Maestro, Oregon Trail, Early Sweet, Olympia
  Soup Peas: Capucijiner's, Bill Jump's Soup, Holland Brown

FLOWERS

These hardy flowers grow like weeds. Hardy annuals are some of the most useful plants for the organic flower gardener. They effectively fill in spots between new plantings of perennials and shrubs. They will not stop the growth of weeds, but will often overcome less-desired weeds. And who could deny the beauty of the vibrant colors supplied by these hardy annuals?

Hardy Annuals

Alyssum *Lobularia maritima*
Baby's Breath *Gypsophila elegans:* Covent Garden, Red Cloud
Bachelor's Buttons *Centaurea cyanus*
Breadseed Poppy *Papaver somniferum*
California Poppy *Eschscholzia* spp.: *E. californica* var. *maritima, E. caespitosa,* Moonglow, Inferno
California Bluebells *Phacelia* spp.: *P. campanularia, P. parryi,* Tropical Surf
Baby Blue Eyes *Nemophila menziesii*
Corn Cockle *Agrostemma githago:* Milas
Papaver commutatum
Farewell-to-Spring *Clarkia* spp.: *C. amoena, C. bottea, C. deflexa, C. rubicunda, C. unguiculata*

Fried Eggs *Limnanthes douglasii*
Forget-Me-Nots *Myosotis sylvatica*
Johnny Jump Ups *Viola tricolor*
Larkspur *Delphinium ajacis:* Frosted Skies, Imperial Strain
Love-in-a-Mist *Nigella* spp.: Curiosity, Persian Jewels
Lupines, Annual *Lupinus* spp.: *L. nanus, L. densiflorus*
Mountain Phlox *Linanthus grandiflorus*
Rose Angel *Silene coeli-rosea*
Shirley Poppies *Papaver rhoeas:* Mother of Pearl, Angel Wings
Sweet Peas *Lathyrus odoratus:* Cupani, Painted Lady, Royal mix, Bicolor Melody
Toad Flax *Linaria maroccana*

Sow in Cloche

Late Febuary

BEET FAMILY *Chenopodiaceae*
  Beets: Detroit Dark Red, Chioggia, Early Wonder, Kestral
  Spinach: Winter Bloomsdale, Olympia, Skookum
CARROT FAMILY *Apiaceae*
  Cilantro: Large Leaved, Santo (Slo-bolt)
MUSTARD FAMILY *Brassicaceae*
  Arugula/Rocket
  Broccoli Raab: Spring raab
  Cress: Curly, Broadleaf
  Chinese Cabbage: Nerva
  Mustard: Green Wave, Red Giant, Mizuna
  Radishes: Cherry Belle, French Breakfast, Easter Egg, Fluo
  Turnips: Tokyo Market, Ohno Scarlet, White Egg
  Oriental Greens: Pac Choi, Joi Choi, Tah Tsai, Komatsu-na
PURSLANE FAMILY *Portulacaceae*
  Miner's Lettuce
SUNFLOWER FAMILY *Compositae*
  Endive: Frisee, President, Perfect
  Lettuce: Red Sails, Brune d'Hiver, Perella, Rubens Red Romaine, Simpson
  Shungiku
PEA FAMILY *Fabaceae*
  Fenugreek

Sow Indoors to Transplant

Late February marks the beginning of sowing for spring and summer. Most of these crops will not be planted out until April, May or June. The advantage of starting these plants in February and March is that many of them take longer to mature than is possible in the cool summers of the Maritime Northwest. Direct sowing would result in a low harvest. To manage this juggling act of young plants, four points are important to consider:

1) Plants started indoors will need supplementary light. Diffuse sunlight results in poor seedling growth.

2) Most seeds germinate at the highest rate at 60° to 72° F, so some sort of bottom heat is necessary (see Propagation Boxes, pg. 3).

3) Seedlings will need to be transplanted from flats to pots, so be sure to reserve enough space to allow for all the plants sown (see Tips for Transplanting, pg. 27).

4) Half-hardy plants can be planted out in April, but tender plants cannot survive the cool nights, so they cannot be planted out until May and June (see March, pg 20).

VEGETABLES AND HERBS

BEET FAMILY *Chenopodiaceae*
  Good King Henry
BUCKWHEAT FAMILY *Polygonaceae*
  Garden Sorrel
  Rhubarb: Glaskins Perpetual, Victoria
CARROT FAMILY *Apiaceae*
  Celeriac: Brilliant, Diamant, Giant Prague, Dolvi
  Celery: Utah, Red Stalk, Ventura
  Cutting Celery: Heung Kunn, Dinant, Amsterdam Fine, Mitsuba
  Finnocchio: Romy, Perfection
  Parsley: Italian Flat, Gigante D'Italia, Moss Curled, Krausa
ONION FAMILY *Alliaceae*
  Chives: Grolau, Pink Flowered, Common
  Garlic Chives *Allium tuberosum*
  Broadleaf Chives *Allium senescens*
  Leeks: early tall varieties, Varna, Otina, Splendid, Le Lyon
  Onions: Ailsa Craig, Italian Red Torpedo, Blanco Duro
LILY FAMILY *Liliaceae*
  Asparagus: Conover's Colossal, U.C. 157, Waltham
MUSTARD FAMILY *Brassicaceae*
  Broccoli: Calabrese, Premium Crop, Romenesco, Umpqua, Rosiland, Decicco, Shogun
  Cabbage: Derby Day, Early Jersey Wakefield, Golden Acre, Red Acre, Salarite
  Cauliflower: Early Snowball, Snow Crown, Ravella
NIGHTSHADE FAMILY *Solanaceae*
  Eggplant: Little Fingers, Ichiban, Short Tom, Long Tom, Violetta di Firenze, No. 226, Neon, Orient Express
  Sweet Peppers: Early Cal Wonder, Northstar, Lilac Bell, Gypsy, Banana Supreme, Cubanelle, Marconi, Golden Summit, Antohi's Romanian, Corono di Toro, Klari Baby

Hot Peppers: Super Cayenne, Czech Black, Riot, Sure-fire, Bulgarian Carrot, Early Jalapeno
Slicing Tomatoes: Stupice, Kootenai, Siberian, Oregon Spring, Celebrity, Slava, Saltspring Sunrise, Seattle's Best, Yellow Brandywine, Black Krim, Green Zebra, Mr. Stripey (Tigerella), Persimmon, Dona, Oregon Spring, Muskovich, Gregori's Altai, Early Swedish, Golden Treasure, Glory of Moldova
Cherry Tomatoes: Gardener's Delight, Sweet Million, Yellow Pear, Galina, Sungold, Peacevine, Rose Quartz, Gold Nugget, Principe Borghese
Paste Tomatoes: Monix, Almetia, Viva Italia, Oregon Pride, Milano, Oroma
SUNFLOWER FAMILY *Compositae*
  Endive: Frisee, Perfect
  Dandelion: Montmogny, Ameliore
  Lettuce: Sucrine, Capitaine, Freckles, Fairellenshleusse, Merveille des Quatre Saisons, Reine des Glaces, Brunia

FLOWERS

A resourceful gardener need not pay the price for tiny six-pack annuals at a nursery. A great number of fine tender annuals can be started at home with a simple propagation box providing supplementary heat and light. This list contains the slower growing tender annuals and some half-hardy annuals.

Bee Balm *Monarda* **spp.:** *M. menthifolia, M. citriodora, M. didyma*
Begonia (tubers)
Black-Eyed Susans *Rudbeckia* **spp.**
China Aster *Callistephus chinensis*
Coreopsis lanceolata: Early Sunrise
Cupid's Dart *Catananche caerulea*
Daisies *Chrysanthemum* **spp.:** Primrose Gem, Painted, Hardy Mums
Flowering Tobacco *Nicotiana* **spp.**
  N. alata: Fragrant Cload, Lime Green
  N. sylvestris: Only the Lonely
Hawksbeard *Crepis rubra*
Indian Blanket *Gaillardia* **spp.**
Mallow *Malva sylvestris:* Bibor Felho, Zebrina
Milkweed *Asclepias curassavica:* Sunset, Gay Butterflies Mixed
Mexican Fleabane *Erigeron karvinskianus:* Profusion
Petunia
Phlox *Phlox drummondii:* Dwarf Beauty, Tapestry
Roman Chamomile *Anthemis nobilis*
Rose Campion *Lychnis coronaria*
Snapdragon *Antirrhnum* **spp.:** Rocket White, Peaches and Cream, Black Prince
Sneezeweed, annual *Helenium amarum*
Stock *Matthiola bicornis:* Cinderella, Ten-week Stocks
Tender Salvias *Salvia* **spp.:**
  S. coccinea: Apple Blossom, Coral Nymph
  S. farinacea: Strata, Victoria
Verbena bonariensis
Wax Flower *Cerinthe major* **var.** *purpurascens*
Yarrow *Achillea* **spp.:** Summer Pastels, Colorado

Creating a Child's Garden

Kids, like adults, want plants that are easy to eat, fun to cultivate, or look unusual or impressive. There are many to choose from: cherry tomatoes, snap peas, carrots and lemon cucumbers are ready-to-snack. Excavating potatoes is an adventure, as is mounding the soil around the base of the plants and peeking underground to see how the spuds are growing. Sunflowers grow 3 times as tall as a five-year-old.

Trellising vining crops to create hiding spots and grottoes in the garden is one of the easiest ways to use a garden's endless potential as a grown magic environment. Bean teepees and sweet pea tunnels are excellent hiding spots. Make a topiary bean plant by building a trellis in the shape of a dog, house or the head of a dragon, then plant beans around the base of your structure. Make a cucumber teepee into the skirt of a scarecrow.

See if you can grow a child's favorite food, even if it's bread. A pizza-theme garden could include tomatoes, wheat, basil, oregano, peppers, onions, and alfalfa for the cows. Plant the crops in the shape of a pizza, a circle with slices for each crop and pepperoni stones to walk on. Another theme is a salad quilt, with all the veggies planted in squares by color or shape; or plant an entire garden in a child's favorite color.

Some kids don't like gardening, but they do like insects, in which case you can plant beneficial insect-attracting plants, butterfly plants or put beetle houses around the garden—piles of rocks and brick that provide habitat for beneficial insects and hours of bug hunting.

Whatever way you find for a child to join you in the garden, it is most important not to force a disinterested kid. Lure them in, lay out tantalizing options and surprise yourself—and your child or your neighbor's child—with what a garden can be.

See page 72 , for children's gardening resources.—BW

Join a Community Supported Agriculture (CSA) Farm

Community Supported Agriculture (CSA) is one of the best things to happen to small farms and consumers in many years. A CSA is a local farm that provides fresh produce directly to consumers, usually on a subscription basis. The consumer pays up front in the spring for a share in the season's produce, anywhere from 15-25 weeks worth of food depending on the farm. The farmer provides a variety of fresh, seasonal vegetables directly to the consumer each week, either at the farm or at a "drop site" in the customer's neighborhood.

This is a great situation for both the farmer and the eater. The farmer has money in her pocket in the spring and can focus on growing food rather than marketing. If a crop fails, the customer shares in the loss with the farmer. Conversely, if there is a bumper crop of a certain item, the customer shares the bounty. The eater wins in other ways too. The produce is fresh-picked, of high quality and at the peak of its flavor. Customers learn to eat with the seasons and build a relationship with a local farm and farmer. For a list of CSA's in Western Washington, call the Seattle Tilth office at (206) 633-0451, or dial up our website at www.seattletilth.org.—JJ

Potting Soil Pointers

Soil Mixes for Seedlings

The perfect potting soil supports strong growth and nurtures emerging seedlings. A mix should absorb and hold water, but also drain well and not compact or crust over from frequent watering. Young seedlings have low nutrient needs; the sowing mix need not be rich, but balanced nutrients should be available. For a sowing mix, all ingredients should be sifted through a $1/4$-inch mesh screen. As you grow as a gardener, feel free to adjust the mixes for nutrient source, drainage and water-retention abilities.

BLENDED SOWING MIXES

Basic Sowing Mix

1 part soil or composted sod
1 part leaf mold or moss/thatch compost
1 part sand, granite grit or pumice

This is the standard by which other sowing mixes can be judged. Leaf mold is a Seattle Tilth favorite; but sometimes gardeners must make do with what is available.

Compost Based Sowing Mix

1 part soil or composted sod
1 part weed or yard-waste compost
2 parts mix of granite grit or sand, vermiculite and perlite

If a mix is disproportionately high in compost it has a tendency to crust over with frequent watering. This mix compensates with materials that promote drainage.

Store-Bought Sowing Mix

1 part sphagnum moss or coconut hulls
1 part perlite and vermiculite
$1/2$ part vermicompost (worm castings)
1 part sand or pumice

Add $1/4$ cup lime for each 1 cubic foot of potting soil if sphagnum moss is used. Parts of this mix can be purchased at any garden store. Without the worm castings, this mix does not provide enough nutrients for good seedling growth.

Soil Mix for Transplants

After seedlings establish their first or second true leaves, most can be transplanted to 4-inch pots or flats 4 inches deep. The seedlings will begin to grow rapidly and their nutrient needs will increase. Nutrients can be added to a transplant mix by incorporating an organic seedling starter fertilizer, increasing the vermicompost content of the mix, or by applying organic fertilizer tea every week (see pg. 31).

Another goal of transplanting is to create an extensive, branched root system. The coarse structure of granite grit, sand or pumice helps by forcing the roots to branch. Transplant mixes can also be sifted through a mesh of $1/4$- to $1/2$-inch to allow a mix with larger particles.

The Basic Transplant Mix

1 part soil or composted sod
1 part leaf mold or thatch compost
2 parts granite grit/sand mix or pumice
1 part yard-waste compost and vermicompost (equally mixed)

The Store-Bought Transplant Mix

1 part sphagnum moss or coconut hulls
1 part perlite and vermiculite
1 part sand or pumice
1 part yard-waste compost and vermicompost (equally mixed)

Add $1/4$ cup lime for each 1 cubic foot of potting soil if sphagnum moss is used.

Continued on page 19

February

Continued from page 18

Ingredients for Potting Soil Mixes

Over time, all gardeners need to change and amend their potting soil to suit the conditions of their garden. Here is a list of potting soil ingredients that you can mix and match to find the combination that best fits your needs:

Garden Soil—Good garden soil contributes nutrients in a stable, slow-release form and has a good mineral content. It can contain weed seeds and disease organisms.

Composted Sod—Layers of sod and soil composted at least two years results in a soil with a balanced organic matter and mineral content.

Moss/Thatch Compost—Composted moss and thatch from lawns is an excellent medium that absorbs water and has high organic matter content.

Sphagnum Moss (Peat)—Ripped out of great bogs in Canada, this product is sterile and lacks any nutrients; however, it holds water and is high in organic matter. A rather low pH requires lime to be added to the soil mix. Peat has been found to reduce damping off fungus.

Coconut Hulls—This ground by-product of coconut production acts like peat in the soil mix but has a neutral pH.

Leaf Mold—Piling old leaves in the compost bin is the best way to ensure fine quality potting soil within 1-2 years. In order of quality, the leaves to use are oak, maple, ash and alder. Horse chestnut or walnut leaf mold should not be used for seedlings.

Weed or Yard-Waste Compost—A slow composted yard-waste pile results in a balanced slow-release nutrient source for seedlings.

Vermicompost (Worm Castings)—Very high in water soluble nutrients that are accessible to young plants.

Vermiculite—A form of mica that has been "popped" by intense heat. Mica is a clay-like mineral that absorbs water and nutrients but also drains well.

Granite Grit—A by-product from quarries and mining, it ranges in size from dust to gravel. Particles have irregular corners and seem to stimulate root formation.

Builders Sand—Sharp sand in a large particle size does not pack down easily and aids in drainage. Make sure to buy *washed* mountain sand.

Perlite—An expanded silica rock that does not absorb water. It is extremely lightweight for its size with varying shapes and textures that promote drainage.

Pumice—Volcanic rock of various sizes and shapes that aids in drainage and helps create air cavities in the soil.—CE

Composting with Kids

Compost and soil basics provide good rainy season activities. Start a worm bin for lunch scraps. Each child can begin with his own little bin made from a milk carton, and eventually these can be emptied into a big wooden bin for the family or class. Constructing a worm bin is a good woodworking project. Contact Tilth for building instructions.

Use leaves and weeds to start a yard-waste compost pile. Watch it decompose and take the temperature of the pile each day. How hot can you make the pile and how quickly can you make finished compost?

Use the compost to experiment with growing seedlings. Add varying amounts of compost to potting soil and grow seed starts under lights. Start vegetable transplants in February for planting out in the spring.—BW

March

In the Garden

March's fickle moods toy with the gardener's emotions—the weather can be one day bright and cheerful, the next day full of dark, brooding clouds. If you find yourself flipping longingly through your seed packages on a lion of a rainy day, you can get ready for planting by taking a look at each seed's hardiness rating. Hardy, half-hardy or tender are the classifications used to describe each plant's ability to tolerate degrees of frost or cold. Hardy plants can withstand temperatures that dip below 25° F. Frequently these plants can be sown in the fall to overwinter for spring harvest or bloom. Hardy annuals are also the first plants sown in the late winter or early spring; they include spinach, peas, corn salad, fava beans, some lettuce varieties and numerous annual flowers that are adapted to the mild winters of maritime climates.

Half-hardy annuals vary in their degree of frost tolerance; as a rule most can tolerate temperatures around freezing for a short period of time (a few days), but in order for them to thrive, night temperatures should be in the high 40's to 50's F. Some half-hardy plants are carrots, beets, Chinese cabbage, dill, summer savory, spring broccoli and cauliflower. These plants can be started early to transplant into the garden in April, or protected with a cloche until the weather warms.

Tender plants will be killed by the slightest touch of frost. More important for Maritime Northwest gardeners is that most of these plants originate in sub-tropical climates and therefore love heat, heat and more heat. Maritime Northwest nighttime temperatures are often so cold in the spring that tomatoes grow poorly if planted out before May. Even more heat-dependent crops such as basil, peppers and eggplants frequently cannot be planted out until the first of June. In fact, these plants usually grow better under a cloche all summer long.—CE

March

This month the Chinese celebrate the birthday of Mother Earth. You may want to plant some special seeds on the spring equinox to mark the new season.

Sow Outdoors

Throughout March

The hardiest leafy greens and spring peas can still be sown. Plants germinate slowly this time of year, so be sure to patrol for slugs.

VEGETABLES AND HERBS

ONION FAMILY *Alliaceae*
   Onion Sets (for Green Onions)
CARROT FAMILY *Apiaceae*
   Chervil: Brussels Winter, Turnip Rooted
   Cilantro: Slo-Bolt
   Fennel
   Sweet Cicely
   Parsley: Hamburg Root Parsley
MUSTARD FAMILY *Brassicaceae*
   Arugula/Rocket
   Arugula, Rustic *Arugula sylvatica*
   Cress: Broadleaf, Peppergrass
   Radishes: French Breakfast, Fluo, Easter Egg, White Icicle, Tokinashi
   Turnips: Tokyo Market, Ohno Scarlet, Presto, Orange Jelly, Golden Ball, Yorii Spring
   Oriental Greens: Komatsu-na
BEET FAMILY *Chenopodiaceae*
   Spinach: Tyee, Wolter, Skookum, Olympia
   Swiss Chard: Five-Colored Silver Beet (Bright Lights), Charlotte, Fordhook, Rhubarb, Perpetual Spinach
PEA FAMILY *Fabaceae*
   Fenugreek
   Snap Peas: Cascadia, Sugar Daddy
   Snow Peas: Oregon Giant, Oregon Sugar Pod, Dwarf Grey Sugar
   Shelling Peas: Petit Pois, Waverex, Maestro, Oregon Trail, Olympia
   Garbanzo Beans: Black Kabouli, Chestnut Lentils
FLAX FAMILY *Linaceae*
   Flax, Edible: Golden
PURSLANE FAMILY *Portulacaceae*
   Miner's Lettuce

Late March

The first spuds can go into the ground, as well as the tasty and nutritious Jerusalem Artichoke. These tubers will sprout underneath the soil, getting good growth before they emerge in April.

SUNFLOWER FAMILY *Compositae*
   Jerusalem Artichokes: Dwarf Sunray, Fuseau, Smooth Garnet, Stampede
NIGHTSHADE FAMILY *Solanaceae*
   Potatoes: Bintje, Yellow Finn, Urgenta, Ruby Cresent, Russian Banana, Anna Cheeka's Ozette, Peruvian Blue, Cinnabar, Blue Cloud, Sunset, Rojo, Blossom

FLOWERS

Hardy annuals can be sown in beds for cutting, or to fill in bare spots. Hardy annuals can be sown in areas where bulbs will die back in the late spring.

Hardy Annuals

Alyssum   *Lobularia maritima*
Bachelor's Buttons   *Centaurea cyanus*
Bird's Eyes   *Gilia tricolor, Gilia capitata*
Bishop's Flower   *Ammi majus*
Breadseed Poppy   *Papaver somniferum*
Calendula   *Calendula officinalis*
California Poppy   *Eschscholzia* spp.: *E. californica* var. *maritima, E. caespitosa* Moonglow, Inferno
California Bluebells   *Phacelia* spp.: *P. campanularia, P. parryi,* Tropical Surf
Baby Blue Eyes   *Nemophila menziesii*
Blue Woodruff   *Asperula azurea*
Corn Cockle   *Agrostemma githago:* Milas
Feverfew   *Tanacetum parthenium:* Snowball, Golden *Papaver commutatum*
Farewell-to-Spring   *Clarkia* spp.: *C. amoena, C. bottea, C. rubicunda, C. unguiculata*
Fried Eggs   *Limnanthes douglasii*
Forget-me-nots   *Myosotis sylvatica*
Larkspur   *Delphinium ajacis* Frosted Skies, Imperial Strain
Love-in-a-Mist   *Nigella* spp.: Curiosity, Persian Jewels
Lupines, Annual   *Lupinus nanus, L. densiflorus*
Mountain Phlox   *Linanthus grandiflorus*
Red Maids   *Calandrinia ciliata*
Scarlet Flax   *Linum grandflorum* var. *rubrum*
Shirley Poppies   *Papaver rhoeas:* Mother of Pearl, Angel Wings
Sweet Peas   *Lathyrus odoratus:* Cupani, Noel Sutton, Old Spice Mix, Mrs. R. Bolton
Tick Seed   *Coreopsis tinctoria*
Tidy Tips   *Layia platyglossa*
Virginia Stock   *Malcolmia maritima*

Sow Under a Cloche

Get a jump on spring by sowing half-hardy greens under the protection of a cloche, which speeds up germination and growth. These plants will be ready for harvest three to five weeks before the same plants sown outside in April.

VEGETABLES AND HERBS

CARROT FAMILY *Apiaceae*
   Carrots, Baby: Amsterdam Forcing, Amsdor, Minicor, Thumbelina
   Parsley: Gigante D'Italia, Italian Flat-Leaf, Darki, Krausa
MUSTARD FAMILY *Brassicaceae*
   Arugula/Rocket
   Broccoli: Calabrese, Premium Crop, Romenesco, Umpqua, Rosiland, Decicco, Shogun

Broccoli Raab: Spring Raab

Cabbage: Early Jersey Wakefield, Golden Acre, Red Acre, Salarite, Derby Day

Chinese Cabbage: Nerva

Mustard: Green Wave, Red Giant, Mizuna

Radishes: Cherry Belle, French Breakfast, Fluo, Easter Egg, White Icicle

Oriental Greens: Pac Choi, Joi Choi, Tah Tsai, Komatsu-na

BEET FAMILY   *Chenopodiaceae*

Beets: Detroit Dark Red, Chioggia, Early Wonder, Kestral

SUNFLOWER FAMILY *Compositae*

Endive: Frisee, President, Perfect

Lettuce: Deer Tongue, Red Ridinghood, Drunken Woman Fringe-Headed, Mascara, Bronze Arrow, Simpson, Freckles, Capitaine, New Red Fire

Salsify

Scorzonera

Shungiku

Sow Indoors to Transplant

Do not despair if long-season summer vegetables were not sown last month, as there is still ample time. Anything that was appropriate to sow in February can still be sown. Though a propagation box is still helpful, many gardeners find a truly bright windowsill a satisfactory place to start transplants.

VEGETABLES AND HERBS

ONION FAMILY   *Alliaceae*

Chives: Grolau, Pink Flowered, Common

Garlic Chives   *Allium tuberosum*

Broadleaf Chives   *Allium senescens*

Leeks (early, tall varieties): Varna, Otina, Splendid, Le Lyon, Sherwood

Green Onions: Evergreen White, Ishikuri Long, Red Beard, Welsh Onion, Kincho Long

CARROT FAMILY   *Apiaceae*

Celeriac: Brilliant, Diamant, Giant Prague, Dolvi

Celery: Utah, Red Stalk, Ventura

Cutting Celery: Heung-Kunn, Par-cel, Dinant, Amsterdam Fine, Mitsuba

Finnocchio (bulbing fennel): Romy, Perfection

Parsley: Italian Flat, Gigante D'Italia, Moss Curled, Krausa

MUSTARD FAMILY   *Brassicaceae*

Broccoli: Calabrese, Premium Crop, Romenesco, Umpqua, Rosiland, Decicco

Cabbage: Early Jersey Wakefield, Golden Acre, Red Acre, Salarite, Derby Day

Cauliflower: Early Snowball, Snow Crown, Ravella

Crambe maritima

BEET FAMILY   *Chenopodiaceae*

Good King Henry

New Zealand Spinach

BUCKWHEAT FAMILY   *Polygonaceae*

Garden Sorrel

Rhubarb: Glaskins Perpetual, Victoria, Champagne Series

MINT FAMILY   *Lamiaceae*

Anise Hyssop   *Agastache foeniculum, A. rugosa*

Marjoram   *Origanum × marjoricum*

Summer Savory

Perilla

Lemon Anise Hyssop   *Agastache mexicana*

Lemon Balm

NIGHTSHADE FAMILY   *Solanaceae*

Sweet Peppers: see February Listings

Hot Peppers: see February Listings

Slicing Tomatoes: see February Listings

Cherry Tomatoes: see February Listings

Paste Tomatoes: see February Listings

Tomatillo: Indian Strain, Purple de Milpa

Ground Cherry: Cape Gooseberry, Aunt Molly's, Sweet Amber

Garden Huckleberry: Burbank's Garden Huckleberry

FLOWERS

When planning the vegetable garden, don't forget to add flowers that will feed beneficial insects (see pg. 41), and provide food for the human soul.

African Daisy   *Arctotis* spp.

Begonia   (tubers)

Bolero Flower   *Salpiglossis sinuata*

Butterfly Flower   *Schizanthus × wistonensis*

China Aster   *Callistephus chinensis*

Chinese Forget-me-not   *Cynoglossum amabile*

Chinese Lantern   *Physalis alkekengi*

Cupid's Dart   *Catananche caerulea*

Lion's Tail   *Leonotis nepetaefolia:* Staircase

Livingstone Daisy   *Mesembryanthemum* spp.

Lobelia erinus: Crystal Palace, Rosamond, Fountain series

Mallow   *Malva sylvestris:* Bibor Felho, Zebrina

Marigold   *Tagetes* spp.

    African   *T. erecta:* Crackerjack, Pinwheel

    French   *T. patula:* Legion of Honor, Naughty Marieta

    Gem   *T. signata:* Lemon, Tangerine, Golden, Paprika

Mignonette   *Reseda odorata*

Monarch of the Veldt   *Arctotis fastuosa:* Zulu Prince

Orange Cosmos   *Cosmos sulphureus*

Phlox   *Phlox drummondii:* Dwarf Beauty, Tapestry

Pincushion Flower *Scabiosa atropurpurea:* Ace of Spades

Statice   *Limonium* spp.

    L. sinuatum: Rainbow, Sunset Shades

    L. sinense: Stardust

Strawflower   *Helichrysum* spp.

Swan River Daisy   *Helipterum rodanthe*

Stock   *Matthiola bicornis:* Cinderella, Ten-week Stocks

Zinnia spp.

    Z. angustifolia: Star Bright, Electric Orange

    Z. elegans: Pinwheel, Blue Point

    Z. haageana: Persian Carpet, Old Mexico

Your Living Bank

Organic matter and nutrients provided through compost and composted manures are the primary sources of fertility for an organic garden. The organic matter decomposes into humus, a constantly changing chaos teeming with millions of organisms per spoonful.

To simplify things a bit, think of the humus in the soil as a living bank. A gardener builds up reserves in the soil by adding compost and digging in cover crops that will be "withdrawn" by growing crops. Organic matter reserves make up a small percentage of the soil. Though the ideal percentage varies, for most vegetable gardens the soil should contain from 4 to 10 percent organic matter. Relative to other soil components, the humus bank's important functions far outweigh this small percentage.

MAKING A DEPOSIT

Humus assists in the creation of soil structure or tilth. After a few years of adding compost to a garden, good soil structure is evident in soil particles holding together in aggregates that crumble apart when the ground is worked. This crumb structure increases pore space within the soil, increases the soil's air content and improves its ability to receive and hold water.

High humus content allows for beneficial organisms to thrive and reduces disease organisms. In particular, soil microrhizal fungi proliferate. These beneficial fungi live in the soil and invade the root hairs of plants. This may sound threatening, but the fungi develop a symbiotic relationship with the plant. They provide small amounts of mineral nutrients that the plants cannot take up by themselves, and receive carbohydrates in return.

Humus added through composts and composted manures often supplies adequate amounts of trace minerals important to plant metabolism. It also reduces the loss of mineral nutrients due to leaching from excessive rain or irrigation. The complex microorganisms and chemical bonds within humus hold nutrients in a living matrix.

The humus bank provides a natural, slow-release nutrient source for crop plants.

WITHDRAWING FROM THE HUMUS BANK

To withdraw from the bank and provide nutrients for growing plants, humus must go through a process called mineralization. Soil bacteria break down more complex organisms, and in the process release nutrients in a water-soluble form that plant roots can absorb. Mineralization requires soil life, air, moisture, mineral nutrients and warmth.

The gardener assists the process of mineralization by digging, cultivating and watering the soil during the appropriate season.

Soil warmth is probably the most overlooked factor in Northwest gardens. A whole book could be written on the relationship between cold, wet soils and nutrient availability. Increased soil warmth is what signals the so-called growing season. The soil warms and soil life increases, resulting in more nutrients being made available to plants. Gardeners attempt to extend the growing season by extending the time the soil is warm, using cloches, cold frames, propagation boxes and greenhouses.—CE

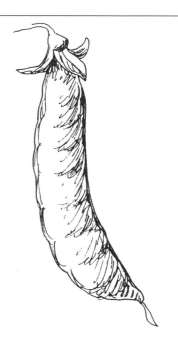

Organic Fertilizers or Soil Amendments

Maritime Northwest soils generally do not have adequate reserves of mineral plant nutrients to grow a healthy and productive garden. This poor soil condition is a function of how these soils were formed, our infamous weather and human disturbance.

In particular, most Maritime Northwest soils are low in organic matter, and are therefore low in nitrogen. The parent rock that made most Northwest soils is low in phosphorus and calcium, and the soil sulfur content is low due to excessive winter rainfall.

The purpose of soil amendments is to provide missing nutrients for the first few years, and to build long-term reserves, thereby reducing the need for soil amendments.

Organic soil amendments are made from either previously living organisms or are mined from the Earth. The three large numbers on fertilizer bags represent the percentages of available nitrogen, phosphorus and potassium, respectively. For example, Fish Meal with 10 percent available nitrogen, 5 percent available phosphorus and 2 percent available potassium will be labeled 10-5-2.

The water-insoluble nutrients frequently are not reported on the bag, but through organic gardening practices, these nutrients will be available in subsequent years. As a general rule, consider that half of the total nutrient content will be available the first year, 50 percent of the remaining nutrients will be available the next year, and so on.

Other macronutrients such as calcium, magnesium and sulfur, and micronutrients or trace minerals, are also difficult to locate on organic fertilizer labels. These components help plants regulate metabolism, store nutrients and develop good disease resistance. High quality fertilizer manufacturers usually list the trace minerals.

GENERAL VEGETABLE FERTILIZER RECIPES

Here are two starter recipes for new gardens that provide balanced nutrients. No general recipe or pre-mixed fertilizer should be used year after year without a soil test (see September, pg. 57) to determine the soil's specific needs.

Steve Solomon's Not-So-Secret Organic Fertilizer Formula*

4 parts fish or seed meal
1 part dolomite limestone
1 part rock phosphate or $1/2$-part bone meal
1 part kelp meal
Apply approximately 4 pounds per 100 square feet per crop.

Vegan's Dream Fertilizer Recipe

5 parts alfalfa meal
2 parts rock phosphate
1 part kelp meal
1 part granite dust
Add approximately 5 pounds per 100 square feet per crop.

Count yourself a lucky gardener because the Maritime Northwest is home to numerous companies that provide pre-mixed organic fertilizers. The fertilizers are usually of very high quality. Frequently the fertilizers come in pellets, which reduce the amount of dust to breathe while spreading fertilizer. Read all the labels carefully to determine which fertilizer you need and how much to use. (See Resources, pg. 72.)—CE

*Reprinted with permission from *Growing Vegetables West of the Cascades* by Steve Solomon, Sasquatch Books, 1989.

March

120- (or so) Ingredient Salads

"Wild" salads contain all the vitamins, minerals, enzymes, trace nutrients and "stimulating bitters" that the body needs. Another attribute is a delightful sequence of *differently* flavored bites. Chewing through the bowl becomes a thrilling sensory experience. One mouthful may be chiefly onion, the next bite, crunching radish, the next, hot sage or cool corn salad. The rich mixture of leaf colors, sizes and textures is reflected in the flavors. My salads have normally at least 30 ingredients; 70 is the usual limit; over 125 the record. Over the years I've used more than 300 plants in salads. The goal is to use as many fresh ingredients as possible, with minimal dressing. Fresh means picked the day the salad will be eaten, or as soon as possible beforehand.

Try not only the obvious, familiar crops, but also culinary herbs, wild plants and some fresh tree leaves. I eat some ingredients which taste bitter or acrid, or are fuzzy or slimy—knowing that though they may be less than gratifying to the tongue, they are healthy for the body. And what may be repulsive by itself can be acceptable in a mixed salad—bitter dandelion and chicory, acrid dame's violet and rough comfrey to name a few. Many ingredients are used only in minute amounts. To make a palatable salad, select according to the available plants and the mixture of flavors and textures.

After eating a salad of dozens of strikingly different fresh plants for the first time, people often report new digestive sensations. The herbs I use are frequently tonic, stimulating and mildly active medicinally. At the very least, a few flavorful burps often result.

A critical note: some of us are allergic to certain plants. If you don't know whether you're allergic to a plant, sample a small amount before eating a full serving.

Another word of caution: don't eat plants if you are not *sure* of their identity and edibility.

Salads can be ruined by too much dressing; some salads require no dressing at all to be delicious. If fuzzy leaves and astringent herbs are used, a salad needs dressing. If it is high in crunch, mucilage and succulent textures that are easy on the tongue, it will be good with little or no dressing.

Here are some example plants, the parts to eat and what they taste like:

Allium **Elephant Garlic**
Leaves and flowers; intense garlic flavor

Begonia spp. and hybrids **Begonia**
Flowers; they're delicious, sorrel-like

Bellis perennis **Lawn** or **English Daisy**
Flowers; mildly sweet

Cardamine oligosperma **Wild cress** or **Shotweed**
Tips of the stems and flowers; pepper flavored

Fœniculum vulgare **Fennel**
Whole plant; licorice flavor on robust weedy plant

Mahonia or *Berberis nervosa* **Low Oregon Grape**
Flowers and tender young leaves; sour

Mentha piperita **Peppermint**
Leaves; all mints are edible, this is choice

Polygonum odoratum **Vietnamese Cilantro** or **Rau Ram**
Young tender leaves; spicy, hot

Portulaca oleracea **Purslane**
Leaves, flowers, seeds; weakly lemony, slimy

Pseudosasa japonica **Arrow** or **Yadake Bamboo**
Peel and eat the shoots in spring and summer; mild anise flavor

Rumex scutatus **French Sorrel**
Leaves; the best sorrel, pretty and easily grown; sour flavor

Satureja montana **Winter Savory**
Leaves; hot spicy flavor available all year

Sedum sarmentosum **Stonecrop**
Leaves; succulent, of little flavor with a pleasing crunch

Solidago odora **Sweet** or **Anise Goldenrod**
Whole plant; warm, rich flavor like tarragon

Sonchus oleraceus **Sow-thistle**
Leaves and stems; mildly bitter dandelion cousin

Stellaria media **Chickweed**
Whole plant except roots; mild flavor, somewhat like lawn clippings

Tropæolum majus **Nasturtium**
Leaves and flowers; hot zesty, peppery flavor

Viola tricolor **Johnny Jump Up** or **Heart's-ease**
Flowers; taste like wintergreen candy

—ALJ

The Naked Gardener on Weeding: A New Twist

The last weekend in May found me trying to catch up with the growth in the garden. After frequent rain, sunshine and several weekends of scant attention from me (due to pressing business in the mountains and other places), the spirit of nature had taken the upper hand in my own backyard and was whipping up unabashed revolt among the local flora. It was biomass on a massive scale. I spent almost the entire three-day weekend paying for my neglect. There was a huge volunteer comfrey plant that could have hidden several members of the Tilth Steering Committee (I checked, they weren't there). There was grass and chickweed and foxgloves and mint and something that might or might not be flea-bane, I just don't know. It all had to come out, to give those things I had actually planted a chance to grow.

This was a few hours of peasant labor (as opposed to pleasant labor). There are other ways of weeding a garden. My wife, for example, likes to weed by accident. This is a very specialized approach, and one I would not necessarily recommend to just anyone. Inadvertent weeding has its risks. Being improperly dressed, for one. I don't know why her crouching in a short skirt should seem more risqué than my naked gardening, but somehow it seems to be.

Her technique is to stride into the garden, improperly dressed, with no apparent intention of doing anything more than cutting some flowers or retrieving something forgotten. Ideally you should look as though you are just on your way somewhere else. This way you catch the weeds unawares. You pause to stoop and pull a weed. Then another, and another. The lack of preparation means that you have nothing to put them in, so they lie in little heaps around the garden. Pretty soon you've been out there for an hour or two, perpetually on your way somewhere else, but persistently pulling weeds. Then you can leave with your flowers, or parsley. If you're lucky some naked gardener fellow will come by later and pick up all the little heaps of yellowing weeds, and put them into the compost heap. You can cut grass this way, too, but you have to use scissors.—NG

Help Preserve Farm Land

In 1997, the American Farmland Trust pronounced farm land in the Puget Sound region of Washington and the Willamette Valley of Oregon among the nation's 10 most threatened farming areas due to pressure for development. Since 1969, the Puget Sound area has lost more than 50,000 acres of farm land to development. In 1979 King County residents approved a bond issue worth $50 million to purchase the development rights of approximately one-quarter of the farm land acres in King County. However, as pressure for new housing and shopping malls builds, ev en some of these "pre-served" areas are at risk. Good farm land and wide open pastures will soon become fields of asphalt if we do not pay attention.

The Puget Sound Farm Trust seeks to preserve farm land in the Puget Sound region, to keep it in active farming and to support sustainable methods of agriculture. You can become a member or donor to this organization and be kept up to date about pending political actions that affect farm land in the region by calling (206) 767-7334.

In addition, consumers can seek out and buy local farm products at farmer's markets or through a community supported agriculture farm (CSA) to help assure markets for local farmers' goods. For a list of CSAs in Western Washington, call the Seattle Tilth office at (206) 633-0451, or dial up our website at www.seattletilth.org.—JJ

April

In the Garden

The weather has begun to settle down a bit, and most areas in the Maritime Northwest are frost free by mid-April. This is the time to pull small weed seedlings before they go quickly to seed. Working between crop plants with a hoe or small hand fork is important not only to get rid of weeds, but also to bring air into the soil, which helps microorganisms provide nutrients to plants and reduces soilborne diseases.

Pricking out seedlings from sowing flats to pots and transplanting seedlings to the garden usually takes up a lot of time this month. Though there are as many techniques for transplanting as there are gardeners, here are a few tips:

- A seedling is usually large enough to prick out when it has two or three true leaves.

- Choose pots that will accommodate the growth of the plant. Many plants can tolerate very shallow pots but will thrive in 4-inch pots or flats 4 inches deep. Plants that will be in pots a long time, such as tomatoes and eggplants, may need to be moved up to gallon pots before being planted out.

- Prick out and transplant in the afternoon or evening. Plants transpire (lose water) during the day, and close their stomata (small orifices located underneath the plant's leaves and along the stem where oxygen and water are released) and metabolize nutrients at night. Transplants need to minimize water loss, and a night of rest helps them to recover.

- Handle small seedlings by their seed leaves, or cotyledons. When the plant matures these leaves will fall off, so if they are damaged in transplanting less harm is done than if the stem is damaged, which the plant needs its whole life.

- Dig a hole big enough to fit the roots without bunching them.

- Water the seedling well with lukewarm water, and try not to get the leaves wet. When a seedling is pricked out, it goes into shock and closes its stomata to avoid water loss; wetting the leaves triggers the opening of the stomata. Place the transplants in the shade for a few days to minimize transpiration and water loss.—CE

April

April

"When April blows her horn, it's good for hay and corn." Even if there's no thunder, the Northwest rains will fill the void.

Sow Outdoors

VEGETABLES AND HERBS

Throughout April

Most half-hardy vegetables can be sown outside in the garden. The cool weather and frequent mild April showers make slow-germinating seeds of root crops easy to grow. In fact, most half-hardy plant seedlings practically leap from the soil.

ONION FAMILY *Alliacaae*

Chives: Grolau, Pink Flowered, Common

Garlic Chives *Allium tuberosum*

Leeks (overwintering varieties): Durabel, St. Victor, Giant Musselburgh, King Richard, Scotland, Unique

Green Onions: Evergreen White, Ishikuri Long, Red Beard, Welsh Onion, Kincho Long

CARROT FAMILY *Apiaceae*

Caraway

Carrots: Touchon, Bolero, Danvers, Nantes Coreless, Scarlet Nantes

Chervil: Brussels Winter, Turnip Rooted

Cilantro: Slo-Bolt (Santo)

Dill: Dukat, Bouquet, Fernleaf

Fennel

Lovage

Parsnip: The Student, All American, Hollow Crown, Tender and True, Andover

Parsley: Gigante D'Italia, Krausa, Darki, Italian Flat-Leaf

MUSTARD FAMILY *Brassicaceae*

Arugula/Rocket

Broccoli: Romenesco, Decicco, Shogun, Umpqua, Thompson

Brussels Sprouts: Vincent, Catskill

Cress: Broadleaf, Peppergrass

Kohlrabi: Purple Vienna, White Vienna, Superschmelz, Rapid

Radishes: French Breakfast, Fluo, Easter Egg, White Icicle

Turnips: Tokyo Market, Ohno Scarlet, Presto, Orange Jelly, Golden Ball, Yorii Spring

Oriental Greens: Kai-laan, Joi Choi, Mei Qing Choi

BEET FAMILY *Chenopodiaceae*

Beets: Crosby's Egyptian, Chioggia, Forono, Intermediate Yellow Mangel, Detroit Dark Red, Bull's Blood, Mac Gregor's Favorite

Orach: Red

Spinach: Nordic, Mazurka, Olympia, Steadfast, Indian Summer, Bloomsdale Long Standing

Swiss Chard: Five-Colored Silver Beet (Bright Lights), Charlotte, Fordhook, Rhubarb, Perpetual Spinach

Quinoa: Faro, Dave, Multihued

SUNFLOWER FAMILY *Compositae*

Burdock (Gobo): Sakigaki, Takinogawa Long, Watanabe Early

Lettuce: Lettuce: for mesclun mixes try Valeria, Lollo Rossa, Oakleaf, Rossa d'Amerique, Mascara, Rougette, Slo-bolt, Brunia

Jerusalem Artichokes: Dwarf Sunray, Fuseau, Smooth Garnet, Stampede

Salsify

Scorzonera

Shungiku

PEA FAMILY *Fabaceae*

(all peas sown in April and beyond should be pea-enation virus resistant)

Snap Peas: Cascadia

Snow Peas: Oregon Giant, Oregon Sugar Pod

Shelling Peas: Maestro, Oregon Trail, Olympia

MINT FAMILY *Lamiaceae*

Anise Hyssop *Agastache foeniculum, A. rugosa*

Chinese Artichokes *Stachys affinis*

Marjoram *Origanum × majoricum*

Summer Savory

Perilla

Lemon Anise Hyssop *Agastache mexicana*

Lemon Balm

MALLOW FAMILY *Malvaceae*

Malva verticillata, Malva crispa, Malva sylvestris

BUCKWHEAT FAMILY *Polygonaceae*

Garden Sorrel

NIGHTSHADE FAMILY *Solanaceae*

Potatoes: Bintje, Yellow Finn, Urgenta, Ruby Cresent, Russian Banana, Anna Cheeka's Ozette, Peruvian Blue, Cinnabar, Blue Cloud, Sunset, Rojo, Blossom

Late April

After the last frost, a different group of plants can be sown outside. These plants can take a late surprise of light frost, but no extremely cold weather. Some of these plants also require higher soil temperatures to germinate out in the garden, which April usually provides. For those who get an early start sowing the winter garden, some long-season cabbages can be sown.

MUSTARD FAMILY *Brassicaceae*

Cabbage (long season fall and winter varieties): Rougette, January King, Savonarch, Danish Ballhead, Chieftain Savoy, Amager

PEA FAMILY *Fabaceae*

Scarlet Runner Beans: Scarlet Emporer, Black Knight, Best of All (Scarlet Runner), Painted Lady, Magic Beans

BEET FAMILY *Chenopodiaceae*

Lambsquarters: Magentaspreen

PURSLANE FAMILY *Portulacaceae*

Purslane: Goldberger, Garden Large-Leaf

FLOWERS

Hardy annuals that tolerate warmer summer temperatures when blooming can be sown throughout April.

Hardy Annuals

Blueweed   *Echium vulgare*
Bishop's Flower   *Ammi majus*
Borage   *Borago officinalis*
Baby Blue Eyes   *Nemophila menziesii*
Blue Woodruff   *Asperula azurea*
Calendula   *Calendula officinalis*
Feverfew   *Tanacetum parthenium*: Snowball, Golden
Love-in-a-Mist   *Nigella* spp.: Curiosity, Persian Jewels
Mallow   *Malva sylvestris*: Bibor Felho, Zebrina
Nasturtium   *Tropaeolum* spp.: Peach Melba, Alaska, Empress of India, Jewel
Quaking Grass   *Briza maxima*
Red Maids   *Calandrinia ciliata*
Scarlet Flax   *Linum grandflorum* var. *rubrum*
Tick Seed   *Coreopsis tinctoria*

Late April

After the last frost, it's time to sow summer blooming half-hardy annuals that will provide flowers for the most of summer.

Blazing Star   *Mentzelia lindleyi*
Canna Lilies (from rhizomes)   *Canna edulis*
China Aster   *Callistephus chinensis*
Chinese Forget-Me-Not   *Cynoglossum amabile*
Cosmos   *Cosmos bipinnatus*: Sea Shells, Sonata Mix, Purity, Candy Stripe
Creeping Zinnia   *Sanvitalia procumbens*
Flowering Tobacco   *Nicotiana* spp.
  N. alata: Fragrant Cload, Lime Green
  N. sylvestris: Only the Lonely
Lace Flower   *Trachymene coerulea*: Blue and White
Lavatera trimestris: Mont Blanc, Silver Cup, Salmon Beauty
Gladiolus (corms)
Lobelia erinus: Crystal Palace, Rosamond, Fountain series
Monarch of the Veldt   *Arctotis fastuosa* Zulu Prince
Orange Cosmos   *Cosmos sulphureus*
Pale Evening Primrose   *Oenothera pallida*
Pincushion Flower *Scabiosa atropurpurea*: Ace of Spades, Giant Mix
Sunflowers   *Helianthus annus*: Velvet Queen, Italian White, Valentine, Evening Sun, Discovery Mix, Endurance
Zinnia spp.
  Z. angustifolia: Star Bright, Electric Orange
  Z. elegans: Scabiosaflora, Pinwheel, Blue Point
  Z. haageana: Persian Carpet, Old Mexico

Sow Indoors to Transplant

VEGETABLES

Throughout April

These are tender plants that grow quickly when planted out, so there is no reason to start them too early.

NIGHTSHADE FAMILY   *Solanaceae*
  Tomatillo: Indian Strain, Purple de Milpa
  Ground Cherry: Cape Gooseberry, Aunt Molly's, Sweet Amber
  Garden Huckleberry: Burbank's Garden Huckleberry

Late April

Plants in the squash family (*Cucurbitaceae*) do not transplant well and are best sown under a cloche. This technique works well with cucumbers, squash, pumpkins and gourds. Melons are another matter altogether: Sow them inside in peat pots, which allow you to plant the whole pot without disturbing the melon's roots. Peat pots also work for other *Cucurbitaceae*. This is also the time to sow the first crop of basil indoors; earlier sowings generally fail because the plants are transplanted out in weather that is too cold.

SQUASH FAMILY   *Cucurbitaceae*
  Cucumber, Slicing: Lemon, Markermore, Straight Eight, Slicemaster Select, English Telegraph
  Hairy Melon: Tse Kwa
  Melons: Early Chaca, Early Hanover, Extra Early Nutmeg, Sugar Baby, Alaska, Savor
  Pumpkin: Sugar Pie, Jack be Little, Spirit, Howden, Rouge Vif D'Etampes
  Squash, Summer: Sunburst, Crookneck, Black Beauty, Goldrush, Cocozelle, Zuchetta Rampicante, Scallopini, Tromboncino
  Squash, Winter: Delicata, Red Kuri, Table King, Eastern Rise, Sweet Dumpling, Doe, Blue Kuri, Waltham Butternut, Spaghetti
MINT FAMILY   *Lamiaceae*
  Basil: Broadleaf Sweet, Fino Verde, Cinnamon, Siam Queen, Sweet Genovese, Red Rubin

FLOWERS

Tender annual flowers often resent transplanting. These can be sown now in peat pots and planted out into the garden in late May.

Butterfly Flower   *Schizanthus wisetonensis*
Cathedral Bells   *Cobaea scandens*
Flowering Amaranth   *Amaranthus* spp.   Love Lies Bleeding, Joseph's Coat
Globe Amaranth   *Gomphrena* spp.
Job's Tears   *Coix lacryma-jobi*
Mexican Sunflower   *Tithonia rotundifolia*: Torch
Morning Glory   *Ipomoea* spp.: Cardinal Climber, Heavenly Blue, Purpurea Mixed
Spider Flower   *Cleome spinosa*: Violet Queen, Helen Campbell, Rose Queen

Cultural Technique: Hardening Off

Plants coddled and tenderly raised indoors or under a cloche need to be slowly acclimated to the outdoor environment. The garden environment will expose the plant to wind that can dry leaves, direct sunlight that can scorch them, and lower temperatures that can slow down or impede growth.

A good general reference is to imagine what it feels like to be a plant. When hardening off, it's important to remember that plants have evolved without legs, so moving them even small distances comes as a great shock. Though the re-acclimatization time varies for different crops, gradual exposure to a new home in the elements will reduce shock for all plants.

Plants raised indoors under artificial lights or on a windowsill are the most tender. Plants too quickly exposed to full sunlight can develop scorched leaves that turn a pale white.

Hardening off requires three weeks to a month for tender plants such as peppers, tomatoes and eggplants. They do best if moved from indoors into a cold frame, and from the frame into a cloche, until they are finally ready for planting out into the garden. However, if you do not have season extending devices you can still harden off plants. Bring the plants outdoors for gradually lengthening periods of time, til at the end of three weeks the plants are out all night.

To harden off these tender plants, set them out in the gentle morning or evening light, or expose them to filtered sunlight on cloudy days. Gradually increase the amount of sunlight they receive over a week's time, until they are exposed to sunlight all day long. To expose the plant to wind and rain, increase the amount of time the frame or cloche is open or vented during the day.

A cloche is very handy to harden off half-hardy plants to be transplanted into the garden. Set the plants out under the cloche, and over a one-week period open the cloche for increasing lengths of time. At the end of the week the cloche can be removed and the plants are ready for the garden.

If no cold frame or cloche is available, choose a nursery area in the garden that receives good sunlight but is somewhat protected from harsh winds. Over two week's time, gradually expose the plants to greater lengths of sunlight and nighttime cold. At the end of this period, the plants are ready to go to their permanent home in the garden. Half-hardy annuals can be hardened off in April. Tender plants can be planted out under a cloche in May, but without a cloche, outdoor planting may need to be delayed until June.—CE

Organic Liquid Fertilizers

In an organic garden, soil temperature is an important factor in helping microorganisms make nutrients available to plants. In the low soil temperatures of spring, soil organisms slow down and make fewer nutrients available to plants. Liquid fertilizers are one way to provide water-soluble nutrients to plants under such adverse conditions. Liquid fertilizers can be served as a tea to the soil or applied as a foliar fertilizer, which is sprayed directly onto the leaves.

Teas are useful for heavy spring feeders such as garlic, shallots, leeks, cabbage, broccoli and cauliflower or cut-and-come-again crops such as spinach and mesclun mixes. The tea is applied once a week to plants in full growth.

Liquid fertilizers also work well for growing heat-loving summer crops like tomatoes, peppers and squash. If the summer is cold and wet, teas help to reduce transplant shock and provide nutrients.

Teas are useful for transplants and plants in pots to compensate for the shock of transplanting or restricted root growth. For transplants, apply teas twice a week at weaker dilutions than for plants already in the ground.

All homemade teas achieve their best aerobic decomposition if they are stirred once or twice a day. Think of this as a fertility meditation time.

Pre-formulated Teas—A recent development in organic fertilizers, these teas include blood meal, bone meal and mined sulfate of potash, which are aerobically digested in water with injected oxygen. There are many products on the market, but one of the best is called Omega; its nutrient content is 7-7-7.

Fish Emulsion—A liquid product of ground up fish waste in water, Fish Emulsion is available in most garden stores. Its nutrient content is 5-1-1, which is a little low in phosphorus and potassium, but provides a good supply of water-soluble nitrogen.

Manure Tea—This homemade mix is created by filling a burlap feed sack half full with fresh manure. Immerse the sack in a garbage can filled with at least 25 gallons of water. The tea is ready when it reeks—in approximately 7 to 21 days. Dilute the tea (1 part tea to 4 parts water) and stir well. Manure tea's nutrient content depends on the type and quality of manure used.

Kelp—Cold-processed kelp provides only small amounts of nutrients and trace minerals, but is popular because it provides more than 70 plant growth regulators as well as important growth stimulants. This is a superb foliar spray or tea for small plants, cuttings and transplants. Apply the tea to the soil twice a week around recently pricked out or transplanted seedlings.

Nettle or Comfrey Leaf Tea—This is another homemade mix that is made like manure tea. Make sure the plant leaves are chopped up or well bruised before immersing them in water. These teas provide phosphorus, potassium, calcium, trace minerals and some of the same plant growth regulators as kelp meal. Dilute 1 part tea to 5 parts water. (This tea really reeks.)

Compost Tea—Compost tea has been proven to reduce damage from leaf fungal diseases such as mildew and rust. To make compost tea, use mature compost that smells of a deep forest floor. Fill a burlap sack half full of the compost and immerse it in 25 gallons of water. Stir well every day, and in one to two weeks the tea will be ready. Dilute from 1:3-1:10 with water.—CE

Salad Mixes

In recent years, it has become en vogue to sow seeds of mixed greens simultaneously in one bed. Although new to most Americans, people have been gathering young greens for salads for thousands of years. In the south of France these salad mixes are called mesclun, a name that has been popularized by "yuppie-chow" producers in the U.S.

These greens are harvested when they are very small in a cut-and-come-again style by trimming the tops off to 1 inch with scissors, or by picking the oldest leaves. The plants are left in the ground for future harvests. After harvesting, fertilize your homespun mesclun with a balanced liquid tea once a week throughout the life of the crop. Young greens produce best in a moist garden bed, so provide at least 1 inch of water a week, if nature is not providing.

Sow seeds for salad mixes every two to three weeks from April to August—a September sowing will provide greens all winter long. Experimentation will allow you to find the square footage that provides enough greens to meet your needs. (See April lettuces.)

Many ready-made mixes are available from seed companies. Of particular note is a blend called Provençal—offered by many seed companies—that produces well in early spring and when September-sown to overwinter. Mixes with lots of mustards also do well in the spring and winter; they can be used as braising greens or lightly cooked vegetables, as well as in salads.

Feel free to make your own mixes; this guide lists many greens that work well for cut-and-come-again salads. *The Salad Garden* by Joy Larkcom is an inspiring and reliable source of information on the selection and culture of salad crops.—CE

Floating Row Covers

Floating row covers are fabric sheets that are placed over plants. The fabric allows light and water to enter, but keeps insects out. Not only is the cover useful for insect control, but it also acts as a moderating influence to weather—raising temperatures a few degrees and minimizing the effects of windy conditions. Floating row covers can be purchased at good garden centers and from mail-order catalogs. (See Resources, pg. 73.)

One way to place the cover is to drape the fabric directly over the plants, allowing enough slack so the plants do not face resistance to upward growth. A more effective method is to use the fabric in place of plastic on a hoop cloche frame. With both methods it is important that the corners and edges are secured to the ground with batons or large boards to keep insects outside.

Floating row covers are especially useful in battling cabbage root and carrot rust fly. The adult cabbage root fly emerges from the soil from late April through May (a second generation emerges from late July through August), to lay eggs at the base of cabbage family plants. The young maggot burrows into the crown and large roots. Root damage ruins the taste of root crops and causes leaf crops to wilt on warm sunny days. Some plants survive the damage, but the yield is greatly reduced.

To minimize damage, keep cabbage family plants covered by a floating row cover and make sure that brassicas have been properly rotated so no adult root flies are trapped under the cover.

The adult carrot rust fly emerges in April and produces many generations throughout the growing season (April through September). A bad infestation can ruin the taste of more than 80 percent of carrots, parsnips, celeriac, Hamburg root parsley and root chervil.

To be effective, the floating row cover must be in place during the entire growing season. Check frequently for holes that develop in the fabric and mend small holes with duct tape; larger holes or tears may require new fabric.—CE

The Month of the Slug

As any Maritime Northwest gardener knows, April is the month of the slug. Mild winters and wet springs provide the perfect habitat and food sources to create large populations of slugs. This can be very frustrating, as every vegetable and flower in the spring garden seems to become slug food. To reduce the "vegeage" (that's vegetable carnage), a gardener needs to reduce slug habitat, put up barriers to slug migration, and trap slugs. Slugs prefer moist, cool ground cover to hide out in. Locate the vegetable garden away from evergreen ground covers or place a barrier between ground covers and the garden.

Hunting and Trapping

After limiting the slugs' general habitat, a gardener can begin to hunt and trap the holdouts. Slug hunting should be done at night or very early in the morning; a flashlight is mandatory. Methodically follow any slime trails and look into the foliage of all plants. Slugs can and do burrow into the top 2 inches of soil, so scratch the soil to look for these slugs.

Eggs and juvenile slugs can also be hunted and disturbed. Frequent cultivation of the soil in spring exposes juveniles for removal and damages the eggs. The eggs look like translucent fish roe (approximately 2-4 millimeters in diameter) and are laid in clusters. (Note: Worm eggs are also small and round, but are opaque yellow in color and are rarely laid in clusters.) Cultivation also disturbs the slugs' navigational habits, as they follow their own slime trails to frequent feeding places.

One popular and effective trap is baited with beer. To make a simple beer trap, cut a few 1-inch holes near the top of a 8- or 12-ounce plastic container.

Fill the bottom with 2 inches of beer and place the trap in the soil, keeping at least $1/4$ inch of plastic exposed below the holes. This leaves windows slugs can crawl through, while leaving a protective "ledge" that keeps ground beetles and other beneficial insects from accidentally falling into the trap. Do not change the beer daily because slugs are attracted to dead slugs. When the beer turns sour and no longer smells of yeast, compost the contents, refill and replace the trap.

Slugs can also be trapped under burlap, old boards or overturned pots. Any dark and protected spot lures slugs.

Barrier Methods

Slugs do not like to migrate over dry soil. Northwest spring weather provides a favorable slug habitat, but so does summer irrigation. Surrounding the yard with non-irrigated borders discourages unwanted migrants in summer. Drip irrigation also limits the amount of water on the surface of the soil, making the general summer environment less pleasant to the slug.

The best proven slug barrier is a copper strip, which works on a similar principle to that of the shock that occurs when people rub their feet along shag carpet. The slug gets a slight electric shock moving over the copper, and is therefore disinclined to travel over it.

The strip of copper needs to be at least 3 inches wide, and set up vertically like a fence, not lying on the ground. The copper strip can be attached to a raised bed or length of bender board (available at lumber yards).

Copper barriers should be contiguous, with no gaps where sneaky slugs can get in. Any slugs that are inside the barrier when it is erected will be trapped inside, so it's important to go out at night and remove any trapped slugs before planting out. Also, remove or trim away any foliage crossing the copper, otherwise the slugs will use it as a bridge to dinner.

Remember: Slugs can be very persistent; they don't have much to do all night long except eat.—CE

May

Do as the ancient Celts and "bring in the May" with flowers, green branches and a celebration of the senses—the first days of May promise the coming of summer.

In the Garden

Oh, the summer garden. Visions of baskets brimming with tomatoes, peppers, basil, corn, squash and beans are the archetype of gardening pleasure. Or are these crops the bane of the Maritime Northwest gardener? Most vegetables that fit the picture-perfect summer garden have been traditionally cultivated in *eastern* North America, Mexico or Central America. These climates are blessed (or cursed) with very warm summer day and night temperatures, and summer rainfall.

This is not to say that the traditional fruits of summer gardens cannot be grown, it just takes us a little more planning and some special techniques. Cloches that are no longer needed for half-hardy plants can be used to assist in germinating seeds of direct-sown summer crops like corn and cucumbers. In May, tomatoes can be planted out under a cloche to get a warm, healthy start.

When transplanting peppers, eggplants, basil and celery wait until the first weeks of June, or plant them under a cloche or in a cold frame. Our summers are often not up to the true production of these crops, so they greatly benefit from the protection of a cloche all summer long. Remember to transplant these heat-loving plants into larger pots and keep them inside under bright lights or in a cold frame until the end of May or beginning of June.

Special care must be taken to properly harden off young transplants of summer crops. Take time to harden them off and do not rush the process of moving them from a warm, protected environment into garden beds.—CE

Sow outdoors

Many tender annuals can be sown directly into the garden. This is the window of opportunity to sow corn to get it to ripen in the Northwest. Varieties of vegetables that grow well in spring need to be replaced by those appropriate for summer.

VEGETABLES AND HERBS

CARROT FAMILY *Apiaceae*
Caraway
Carrots: Touchon, Bolero, Danvers, Nantes Coreless, Scarlet Nantes, Oxheart, Healthmaster, Mokum
Cilantro: Slo-Bolt (Santo)
Dill: Dukat, Bouquet, Fernleaf
Parsnip: The Student, All American, Hollow Crown, Tender and True, Andover

ONION FAMILY **Alliaceae**
Chives: Grolau, Pink Flowered, Common
Garlic Chives *Allium tuberosum*
Leeks (overwintering varieties): Durabel, St. Victor, Giant Musselburgh, King Richard, Scotland, Unique
Green Onions: Evergreen White, Ishikuri Long, Red Beard, Welsh Onion, Kincho Long

AMARANTH FAMILY **Amaranthaceae**
Amaranth, Grain *A. hypochondriacus*: Burgundy, Golden Grain
Amaranth, Greens (Hinn Choy) *A. tricolor* and *A. lividus*: Coleus Leaf, Red Leaf, Bonfire, Red Chief

MUSTARD FAMILY *Brassicaceae*
Broccoli: Romenesco, Decicco, Shogun, Umpqua, Thompson
Brussels Sprouts: Vincent, Catskill, Rubine
Cabbage: Rougette, January King, Savonarch, Danish Ballhead, Chieftain Savoy, Amager, Portugese Cabbage (Couve de Tronchuda)
Radishes: French Breakfast, Fluo, Easter Egg, White Icicle
Oriental Greens: Kai-laan, Hon Tsai Tai (flowering Purple Pac Choi), Yu Choi, Bouquet (flowering Green Pac Choi)

BEET FAMILY *Chenopodiaceae*
Beets: Crosby's Egyptian, Chiogga, Forono, Intermediate Yellow Mangel, Detroit Dark Red, Bull's Blood, Mac Gregor's Favorite
Lambsquarters: Magentaspreen
New Zealand Spinach
Orach: Red
Spinach: Nordic, Mazurka, Olympia, Steadfast, Indian Summer, Bloomsdale Long Standing
Swiss Chard: Five-Colored Silver Beet (Bright Lights), Charlotte, Fordhook, Rhubarb, Perpetual Spinach
Quinoa: Faro, Dave, Multihued

SUNFLOWER FAMILY *Compositae*
Burdock (Gobo): Sakigaki, Takinogawa Long, Watanabe Early
Lettuce: Deer Tongue, Sierra, Grandpa Admire's, Esmeralda, Lobjoit's Green Cos, Fire Mountain, New Red Fire, Optima

PEA FAMILY *Fabaceae*
Beans, Snap Bush: Dragon Tongue, Provider, Triumph de Farcy, Venture, Roma, Royal Burgundy, Nickel, Slederette, Buerre d' Rocquencourt
Beans, Snap Pole: Blue Lake, Musica, Cascade (Oregon) Giant, Emerite, Cherokee Trail of Tears, Dow Purple Pod, Purple Peacock, Romano
Beans, Dry and Shelling Bush: Black Coco, Flageolet, Lucas Navy, Money, Nez Pierce, Orca (Calypso), Speckled Bays
Beans, Dry and Shelling Pole : Aunt Jean's, Bird's Egg, True Cranberry, Robin's Egg Horticultural, Borlotto, Box
Scarlet Runner Beans: Scarlet Emporer, Black Knight, Best of All (Scarlet Runner), Painted Lady, Magic Beans

GRASS FAMILY *Gramineae*
Corn, Sweet: Ashworth, Golden Midget, Midnight Snack, Rainbow Inca, Seneca Horizon, Double Gem, Precocious, Sugar Buns, Sugar Snow, Seneca Starshine
Corn, Flour: Mandan Bride, Parching Red Mandan, Hooker's
Corn, Pop: Dwarf Strawberry, Tom Thumb, Early Pink, Black Teff

MINT FAMILY *Lamiaceae*
Anise Hyssop *Agastache foeniculum, A. rugosa*
Chinese Artichokes *Stachys affinis*
Marjoram *Origanum × majoricum*
Summer Savory
Perilla
Lemon Anise-Hyssop *Agastache mexicana*
Lemon Balm

NIGHTSHADE FAMILY *Solanaceae*
Potatoes: Bintje, Yellow Finn, Urgenta, Ruby Cresent, Russian Banana, Anna Cheeka's Ozette, Peruvian Blue, Cinnabar, Blue Cloud, Sunset, Rojo, Blossom

PURSLANE FAMILY *Portulacaceae*
Purslane: Goldberger, Garden Large-Leaf

FLOWERS

This is the month to sow flowers that need higher soil temperatures to germinate. These annuals provide the main bloom of August and late summer.

Borage *Borago officinalis*
Blazing Star *Mentzelia lindleyi*
Butterfly Flower *Schizanthus × wisetonensis*
Calendula *Calendula officinalis*
China Aster *Callistephus chinensis*
Cosmos *Cosmos bipinnatus*: Sea Shells, Sonata Mix, Purity, Candy Stripe
Creeping Zinnia *Sanvitalia procumbens*
Flowering Amaranth *Amaranthus* **spp.** Love Lies Bleeding, Joseph's Coat
Globe Amaranth *Gomphrena* **spp.**
Lace Flower *Trachymene coerulea*: Blue and White
Lavatera trimestris: Mont Blanc, Silver Cup, Rose Beauty, Salmon Beauty

Marigold   *Tagetes* spp.
>   African   *T. erecta*: Crackerjack, Pinwheel
>   French   *T. patula*: Legion of Honor, Naughty Marieta
>   Gem   *T. signata*: Lemon, Tangerine, Golden, Paprika

Mexican Sunflower   *Tithonia rotundifolia*: Torch

Monarch of the Veldt   *Arctotis fastuosa*: Zulu Prince

Morning Glory   *Ipomoea* spp.: Cardinal Climber, Roman Candy, Heavenly Blue

Nasturtium   *Tropaeolum* spp.: Peach Melba, Alaska, Empress of India, Jewel

Orange Cosmos   *Cosmos sulphureus*

Pale Evening Primrose   *Oenothera pallida*

Slipper Flower   *Calceolaria chelidonioides*

Spider Flower   *Cleome spinosa*: Violet Queen, Helen Campbell, Rose Queen

Sunflowers   *Helianthus annus*: Velvet Queen, Italian White, Valentine, Evening Sun, Endurance, Discovery mix

Tick Seed   *Coreopsis tinctoria*

Zinnia spp.
>   *Z. angustifolia*: Star Bright, Electric Orange
>   *Z. elegans*: Scabiosaflora, Pinwheel, Blue Point
>   *Z. haageana*: Persian Carpet, Old Mexico

Sow Under Cloche

Though a cloche is not necessary to germinate these seeds, it helps in periods of cool weather. Remember, lack of soil warmth is often the cause of poor germination. Be sure to water the seed bed under the cloche and vent it in the middle of the day.

MINT FAMILY   *Lamiaceae*
>   **Basil:** Broadleaf Sweet, Fino Verde, Cinnamon, Siam Queen, Thai Lemon, Thai, Sweet Genovese, Red Rubin

SQUASH FAMILY   *Cucurbitaceae*
>   **Cucumber, Slicing:** Lemon, Marketmore, Straight Eight, Slicemaster Select, English Telegraph
>   **Melons:** Early Chaca, Early Hanover, Extra Early Nutmeg, Sugar Baby, Alaska, Savor
>   **Pumpkin:** Sugar Pie, Jack be Little, Spirit, Howden, Rouge Vif D'Etampes
>   **Squash, Summer:** Sunburst, Crookneck, Black Beauty, Goldrush, Cocozelle, Zuchetta Rampicante, Scallopini, Tromboncino
>   **Squash, Winter:** Delicata, Red Kuri, Table King, Eastern Rise, Sweet Dumpling, Doe, Blue Kuri, Waltham Butternut, Spaghetti

The Naked Gardener Examines Aphids

I don't know about your garden, but this summer mine has become home to more ladybugs than I have ever seen before in my (disordered) life. This may be due to one of those interesting and mysterious cycles immanent in the natural world, like the 13 and 17-year periodic cicada cycles. More likely it is due to the huge number of aphids living on my fava beans. The aphids appear to have no damaging effect on the favas at all, the crop is heavy and I've been eating them since the beginning of June (the beans, not the aphids; I leave that to the ladybugs). Since both the aphids and I like the beans and the ladybugs like the aphids, I'd say we have achieved a happy symbiosis.

Someone in the local organic gardening community recently observed that you *need* a few aphids and suchlike in the garden, *to attract the predators*. Can there be any more succinct statement of the organic method? It's an utterance containing a world of wisdom.

This cloud of ladybird beetles has given plenty of opportunity to study the life-cycle, preferences and inclinations of the little fellows. I note with interest, for example, that the premature form (larvae), favor the Sweet Cicely and crawl all over it, happily munching aphids until that fateful day when they stop dead in their tracks and decide to turn into something else. This is a mid-life crisis of a most extreme kind. What does it feel like, I wonder, to hear an inner voice telling you its time to glue your head to a leaf and rearrange your body?

The mature ladybugs, on the other hand, show a distinct preference for the fava beans, where they indulge in feasting and riotous sex. I'm not kidding. For every two or three ladybugs crawling about solo—working on their 60-a-day aphid habit—there is a pair enjoying each other's company. They take a long time about it, too. This leads inevitably to clusters of tiny yellow eggs stuck under the leaves, and the whole thing starts all over again. Thanks to lifelong myopia I can observe all this in good focus at a distance of 6 inches or so.—NG

Summer Cover Crops

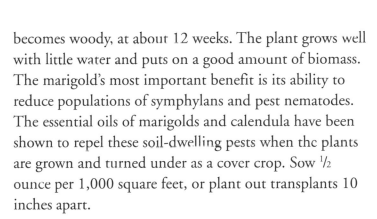

Summer cover crops are very helpful in preparing beds for fall and winter vegetables. They increase available nutrients and add organic matter for crop plants, and some attract beneficial insects. Sow these crops any time from May to the end of July.

Legumes

Berseem Clover—Berseem or Egyptian clover is best sown throughout the spring. A gardener can cut berseem clover twice during the growing season to make compost, then turn the plant under in late summer. After it is turned under as a summer-growing legume cover crop, Berseem will provide nitrogen and organic matter for overwintering brassicas and alliums. The plant can fix up to 300 pounds of nitrogen per acre. Sow 1 pound per 1,000 square feet; alfalfa inoculant is required for good nitrogen fixation. (See pg. 60.)

Bush Beans—Instead of eating the beans yourself, let the soil do the munching. Bush beans mature in 60 days and fix up to 120 pounds of nitrogen per acre; they are useful to grow and turn under in beds planned for winter vegetables with high nutrient needs such as alliums and brassicas. Large bean leaves can help smother weeds if they are cultivated once when they have two to four true leaves. Sow 4 pounds per 1,000 square feet and use a bean inoculant.

Non-Legumes
Buckwheat—This broadleaf annual produces a lot of organic matter and is useful for smothering summer weeds. Buckwheat accumulates mineral phosphorus and when it is turned into the soil, it releases phosphorus in a form crop plants can use. Its flowers are some of the best for providing nectar to beneficial insects. It matures in six to eight weeks, so three to four crops can be grown each summer. Seed at 3 pounds per 1,000 square feet.

Marigold *Tagetes minuta*—This marigold can grow up to 9 feet tall, but is usually turned under before its stem becomes woody, at about 12 weeks. The plant grows well with little water and puts on a good amount of biomass. The marigold's most important benefit is its ability to reduce populations of symphylans and pest nematodes. The essential oils of marigolds and calendula have been shown to repel these soil-dwelling pests when the plants are grown and turned under as a cover crop. Sow ½ ounce per 1,000 square feet, or plant out transplants 10 inches apart.

Bee Bread *Phacelia tanacetifolia*—Bee Bread is commonly grown in Europe as both a cover and honey crop. When thickly sown, the plant grows quickly and smothers weeds. It helps to accumulate calcium and recycle nitrogen that may leach out of the root zones of crop plants. Sow 3 ounces per 1,000 square feet.

Calendula—This plant is the most common summer "weed" at the Seattle Tilth gardens. As a cover crop, calendula outgrows other more invasive and damaging weeds. Turn under the plant about 10 weeks after sowing. The flowers attract beneficial insects and make great cut flowers. Sow 2 ounces per 1,000 square feet.

Perennial Cover Crops and Ley Crops
For gardeners who wish to reduce the amount of fertilizer, compost or manure that needs to be imported into the garden, perennial cover crops and ley crops provide one solution. These crops are sown once and harvested

for compost for a number of years, then finally turned under. Vegetables are then planted in the revitalized bed.

Alfalfa—Alfalfa is one of the highest producers of biomass among temperate-zone herbaceous legumes. A 200-square-foot bed will yield 1 cubic yard of finished compost when mixed 50/50 with a carbon source. In addition to fixing nitrogen, alfalfa has a deep tap root that helps it accumulate phosphorus, calcium, sulfur and trace minerals from the subsoil. Sow alfalfa 1 pound per 1,000 square feet, or plant out transplants 1 foot apart; use an alfalfa inoculant at sowing. Alfalfa needs a neutral pH, adequate phosphorus, sulfur and calcium to thrive.

Bird's Foot Trefoil *Lotus corniculatus*—This plant grows where others fear to tread. It tolerates low fertility, low calcium, poorly drained soils in winter and drought in summer. It's slow to establish, but it is an excellent perennial cover crop for difficult areas. Sow 1 pound per 1,000 square feet. Buy pre-inoculated seed because *Lotus*-specific inoculant is hard to find.

Red Clover, Kenland Red *Trifolium pratense*—Red clover is a short-lived perennial that provides high yields of biomass one year after sowing. To replace nitrogen, it is useful for undersowing (to sow a cover crop while a vegetable crop is still growing) corn, leeks, cauliflower, cabbage or other long-season heavy feeders. Broadcast 1 pound per 1,000 square feet of red clover when the vegetable crop is three-quarters of the way to harvest. Use a clover inoculant. Dig under the clover in spring after it puts on good top growth through the winter. Red clover fixes up to 140 pounds of nitrogen per acre.

Dutch White Clover *Trifolium repens*—White clover is a long-lived perennial that is useful as a nitrogen-fixing ground cover under fruit trees and vines, and works nicely for play areas and pathways. Once established, this clover competes well with weeds and may be a bit aggressive. Sow 1 pound per 1,000 square feet and use a clover inoculant.

Herbal Leys—As well as being healthful for humans, some herbs have been found to accumulate nutrients and trace minerals necessary for plant growth. In traditional agricultures, some herbs were grown to make compost, such as chicory, dandelion, comfrey, nettles, yarrow, sorrel, sheep's parsley and thistles.—CE

Soap Sprays

Soap sprays dry out and kill soft-bodied insects such as aphids, mealy bugs, white flies and mites. These insects are usually not a problem in an organic garden with healthy, fertile soil and plant diversity. However, in a greenhouse, cold frame or cloche where beneficial insects are not present, soap sprays can help lower the populations of these harmful insects. Apply soap sprays before insect damage becomes unacceptable and only if pests are present. Don't use them as preventative maintenance.

Pre-formulated insecticidal soap sprays are made from saponins or potassium fatty acids and differ from household soap. Insecticidal soaps are reasonably priced when purchased as a concentrate and mixed with water.

Spray each plant carefully, covering the tops and the bottoms of the leaves, the growing tips and other places small insects may hide. The soap must smother the insects. After one day, spray the plants with water. Repeat the process after four days. Further applications are necessary only if pest populations rise. If you have repeated problems with pests that require soap spray applications, try to remedy the problem permanently by improving soil health by adding compost.

Note: Soap is toxic to fish and other aquatic species, and should be kept out of all bodies of water.—CE

Edible Plant Sale

Held the first Saturday in May, Seattle Tilth's Edible Plant Sale offrs thousands of plant starts that have been proven to grow and taste great in the Maritime Northwest. Each year more than 30 varieties.

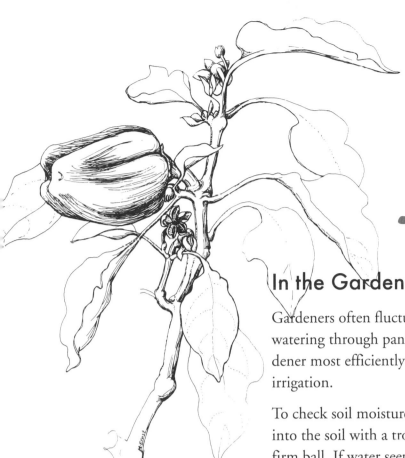

June

In the Garden

Gardeners often fluctuate between under watering through neglect and over watering through panic. How much water is enough and how can a gardener most efficiently irrigate? Here are a few tips to help with summer irrigation.

To check soil moisture, try this hands-on method. Dig down 5 to 7 inches into the soil with a trowel and grab a handful of soil. Squeeze it to make a firm ball. If water seeps out or the soil sticks together, the garden doesn't need water. Toss the ball 6 inches into the air and let it fall into your hand. If it falls apart, the soil needs water.

Not all soils receive and hold water in the same way. Sandy, light soils need less water and more frequent watering—for a total of three-quarters of an inch per week. Heavy, clay soil will accept more water but at less frequent intervals. As the soil becomes more fertile, its water holding capacity increases.

Test sprinklers for how well they cover an area and how much water they put out. A simple test is to set out empty cat food cans around the area to be watered; make sure to sample the whole area— middle, corners and edges. Irrigate for 15 minutes, measure the amount of water in the cans, and multiply by 4 to figure the inches of water applied per hour.

Use a fan or rose attached to a hose when hand watering. Point the head upward and allow a soft sprinkle to fall on a bed of seed you've sown directly into the soil. Be careful not to apply too much water too quickly. The water should land on the soil like a gentle spring rain. Always check the soil to see how deeply the water has soaked in.

Drip irrigation systems and micro-sprinklers reduce evaporation and minimize the leaching of nutrients. These systems are a bit more difficult to maintain, but significantly reduce the amount of time spent hand watering. They are not a panacea for water conservation, nor appropriate for all crops.—CE

June

From North Africa to Scandinavia, the sun is thanked at the end of the longest day of the year with a bonfire at sunset on the summer solstice.

Sow Outdoors

VEGETABLES AND HERBS

Throughout June

The main crop of summer vegetables listed here are cultivars and varieties that produce well in the warmer weather of July and into August. A second crop of some summer vegetables can be sown this month to provide a succession to the May-sown crop.

CARROT FAMILY *Apiaceae*
   Cilantro: Slo-Bolt (Santo)
   Dill: Dukat, Bouquet, Fernleaf
ONION FAMILY *Alliaceae*
   Garlic Chives *Allium tuberosum*
   Broadleaf Chives *Allium senescens*
   Green Onions: Evergreen White, Ishikuri Long, Red Beard, Welsh Onion, Kincho Long
AMARANTH FAMILY *Amaranthaceae*
   Amaranth, Greens (Hinn Choy) *A. tricolor* and *A. lividus*: Coleus Leaf, Red Leaf, Mirah, Bonfire, Red Chief
MUSTARD FAMILY *Brassicaceae*
   Oriental Greens: Kai-laan, Hon Tsai Tai (flowering Purple Pac Choi), Yu Choi, Bouquet (flowering Green Choi)
BEET FAMILY *Chenopodiaceae*
   Lambsquarters: Magentaspreen
   Orach: Red
   Quinoa: Faro, Dave
SUNFLOWER FAMILY *Compositae*
   Lettuce: Deer Tongue, Sierra, Grandpa Admire's, Esmeralda, Lobjoit's Green Cos, New Red Fire, Optima
PEA FAMILY *Fabaceae*
   Beans, Snap Bush: Dragon Tongue, Provider, Triumph de Farcy, Venture, Roma, Golden Roma, Royal Burgundy, Nickel, Slenderette, Buerre d'Rocquencourt
   Beans, Snap Pole: Blue Lake, Musica, Cascade (Oregon) Giant, Emerite, Cherokee Trail of Tears, Dow Purple Pod, Purple Peacock, Romano
PURSLANE FAMILY *Portulacaceae*
   Purslane: Goldberger, Garden Large-Leaf
SQUASH FAMILY *Cucurbitaceae*
   Cucumber, Slicing: Lemon, Marketmore, Straight Eight Slicemaster Select, English Telegraph
   Squash, Summer: Sunburst, Crookneck, Black Beauty, Goldrush, Cocozelle, Zuchetta Rampicante, Scallopini, Tromboncino

Late June

Just when the summer vegetables are really growing, late June rolls around and it's time to start the fall/winter garden. Plan for a nursery bed or flats to grow the long-season winter vegetables sown this month. Many crops can be planted out in the garden as space becomes available. Root crops such as rutabagas, turnips, carrots and beets need to be sown where they will grow as they resent transplanting. Many seed catalogs list varieties that are particularly suited to being grown to harvest in fall and winter. Be open to experimentation, because the companies are constantly introducing new varieties as interest in winter gardening increases.

CARROT FAMILY *Apiaceae*
   Carrots: Shin Kuroda, Kuroda, Fakkel, Bolero, Flakko, Autumn King, Topweight
   Finocchio (bulbing fennel): Zefa Fino
ONION FAMILY *Alliaceae*
   Green Onions: Evergreen White, Ishikuri Long, Red Beard, Welsh Onion, Kincho Long
MUSTARD FAMILY *Brassicaceae*
   Brussels Sprouts: Prince Marvel, Montgomery, Rubine
   Cauliflower: (fall varieties) Alverda, Arbon
   Cabbage: Rougette, January King, Winterstar, Savonarch, Danish Ballhead, Chieftain Savoy, Amager, Rodynda, Portugese Cabbage (Couve de Tronchuda)
   Rutabaga: Marian, Laurentian, American Purpletop
   Turnips: Orange Jelly, Purple Top White Globe, Golden Ball
SUNFLOWER FAMILY *Compositae*
   Endive: Batavian Full Heart, Cornet d'Anjou
   Radicchio: Palla Rossa Especial, Castelfranco, Early Red Trevisio, Giulio
BEET FAMILY *Chenopodiaceae*
   Beets: Lutz Greenleaf, Winterkeeper, MacGregor's Favorite
   Swiss Chard: Five-Colored Silver Beet (Bright Lights), Charlotte, Fordhook, Rhubarb, Perpetual Spinach

FLOWERS

There is still time to sow flowers for late summer bloom; flowers sown now will be at their peak in August and September. Keep the seed bed moist until germination occurs.

Borage *Borago officinalis*
Butterfly Flower *Schizanthus × wisetonensis*
Calendula *Calendula officinalis*
Creeping Zinnia *Sanvitalia procumbens*
Lace Flower *Trachymene coerulea*: Blue and White
Nasturtium *Tropaeolum* spp.: Peach Melba, Alaska, Empress of India
Slipper Flower *Calceolaria chelidonioides*
Spider Flower *Cleome spinosa*: Violet Queen, Helen Campbell, Rose Queen
Sunflowers *Helianthus annus*: Velvet Queen, Italian White, Valentine, Evening Sun, Endurance, Discovery Mix
Zinnia spp.
   Z. angustifolia: Star Bright, Electric Orange

Getting to Know Beneficial Insects

Insects are a natural part of gardening. As you read this, there is a veritable Wild Kingdom of activity happening in your yard, with insects breeding, eating and being eaten. It is comforting to know that 98 percent of the insect species on the planet are beneficial. These insects are out there pollinating crops, working the soil and eating or generally being a nuisance to pest insects.

In an ecologically diverse organic garden, naturally occurring beneficial insects usually adequately control the most common pests such as aphids, thrips, white flies, mites and leaf miners. Think of these pests as the plankton of the garden; they provide food for beneficial insects. Often patience is all that is required—the plant will outgrow the pest problem if you use proper cultural techniques such as building healthy soil and sowing plants at their proper times.

A good hand lens greatly magnifies the fun of looking at the insect life in your garden. Choose a lens with at least 10- to 20-times magnification.

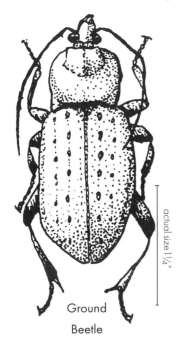

Ground
Beetle

Ground Beetles, Family *Carabidae*—This very common garden insect crawls along the ground eating soil-dwelling pests such as cutworms, root maggots and slug eggs. There are many different ground beetles, the predacious beneficial ones run very quickly and can be identified by the large mandibles on their foreheads.

Lady Beetle Larva

actual size 4/5"

Rove Beetles, *Staphylinidae*—These black beetles have segmented, extended abdomens, which they hold up like scorpion tails when threatened. These ground-dwellers live in garden debris, where they eat cutworms and other soil pests.

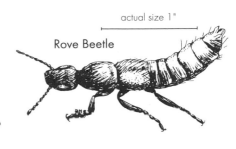

actual size 1"

Rove Beetle

Lady Bugs, Family *Coccinellidae*—With more than 100 species endemic to North America, the convergent lady beetle is one of several that look alike and have similar life cycles. Their orange eggs are laid under leaves near large populations of pests. The larvae look like tiny orange and black alligators, and consume impressive numbers of pest insects. The adults eat insects, but can thrive with adequate nectar sources.

actual size 3/5"

Lady Beetle

Lacewings, *Chrysopa*—Adult lacewings are approximately 1/2-inch long with delicate wings that they hold above their bodies. The adults eat nectar and fly around looking for mates. The larvae are commonly called aphid lions due to their voracious appetite for aphids, mites and small insect eggs. The larvae also grow to be about 1/2-inch long.

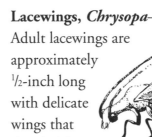

Lacewing

actual size 1/2"

June

Minute Pirate Bug, *Orius*—This important predator often goes unnoticed because it is only ⅛-inch long. The adults and young

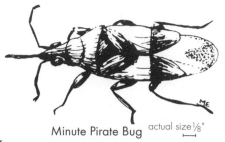

Minute Pirate Bug   actual size ⅛"

alike spear young thrips and other pests, then suck their insides out like a milkshake. Several generations are born during the growing season.

Spiders, *Arachnida*—While not technically insects, all spiders are important pest predators in the garden. Wolf spiders and crab spiders do not spin webs, but instead lie in wait on foliage or debris to jump on their prey. Spiders need some protective plant covering to overwinter in the garden. Cottony spider egg sacs can be found under debris and wood.

Syrphid Fly, Hover Fly, Flower Fly, *Syrphidae*—The adult flower fly looks like a bee and can be seen hovering around flowers as it gathers nectar. The larvae are blind and look a bit like small slugs, but are pale green to brown in color; they feed throughout the growing season on soft-bodied pest insects. A black oily trail of excrement on leaves is an indication of syrphid fly larvae feeding activity.

Syrphid Fly   actual size ¾"

Wasps, Bald-Faced Hornets, Yellow Jackets, *Vespula*—Though these insects do sting and can be an annoyance at picnics, they are welcome predators in the garden. The adults feed on nectar, but capture caterpillars and small insects to feed their young.—CE

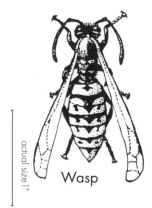

actual size 1"   Wasp

Kid-Smart Garden Art

Garden-based crafts are limited only by our imaginations. The garden is a good resource for materials and makes a great open-air art gallery.

Scarecrows and garden signs can be as easy or as complex as you and a child choose to make them. A plank nailed to a stick, painted and decorated with cloth and baubles, is the simplest scarecrow. Pose more complex, classic scarecrows in funny positions, stuffing clothing with straw and painting a pillowcase head. Making signs for crops is a good winter project, with materials as diverse as wood and oven-baked clay.

Use Plaster of Paris to make basic mosaic tiles (the instructions are on the box). Have all your mosaic supplies ready: broken mirrors, small toys, matchbox cars, old magnets, (sticks and seeds are also nice, but will last only a little while out in the elements). The plaster should be poured into a container with four sides, about 1-2 inches deep. For example, cut a shoe box in half and flip up the open end to create a smaller box. Press your mosaic materials into the plaster. Set aside to dry, and after you peel off the cardboard, place the tiles around the garden.

Make a musical instrument called a rain stick with seeds saved from dried corn, peas, beans or rice. Pick up spare heavy cardboard tubing from a fabric store. Drive nails of an appropriate length in a spiral pattern down the tube; close off one end with cardboard or tape. Fill the tube with the seeds, testing for the sound you like when you tilt the tube up and down, then close off the open end. The seeds falling inside a tube sound like rain. Decorate it by painting, covering it with fabric or gluing seeds to the ends.

A popular activity with younger children is to paint and draw with plants. Collect flowers and leaves of various colors, and delicately mush them about on pieces of paper, experimenting with color and form.—BW

Tomato Late Blight

Phytopthora infestans is a fungus that creates brown or black lesions on your prized tomato plants. The lesions begin on leaf veins, stems and petioles and can spread like wildfire all over the plant and fruit leaving the gardener with a foul-smelling mess. The fungus is transferred from the soil to foliage by splashing water. Common Maritime Northwest summer weather—with cool nights in the 50°s, slightly warmer days in the 60°s or 70°s, and plants wet from rain or irrigation—creates the ideal conditions for this fungus to spore and grow. Do not be disheartened; there are a number of techniques to try before you give up and grow only brassicas.

Crop rotation assists in breaking the disease cycle. After tomatoes have been grown in one area, they should not be planted there again for three to five years. All infected tomato plants should not be composted, but either burned or sent to a disposal site.

An elaborate blight prevention measure involves building a 6-foot-high plastic cloche or tunnel over your tomato patch. The cloche raises the day and night temperatures, and blocks out misty rainfall.

A more practical measure for most gardeners is proper trellising and training of the plants. The goal of trellising is to support the plants and to allow air circulation around the foliage so it dries quickly after rain. The tomato cages sold at garden stores are too small for an indeterminate tomato (though they work for paste and determinate tomatoes fairly well), and result in a tangled mass of plant that traps water and becomes a nursery for fungus spores.

The best trellis is a fence structure with sturdy posts sunk 2 feet in the ground, with horizontal slats placed 6 inches apart up to about 5 feet high. Trellises can also be made of sheep or hog fencing stapled to sturdy posts. Any trellis should be strong enough to support fruit-laden plants and allow excellent air circulation.

The goals of training and pruning tomatoes are early fruit set and increased air circulation. Picture a fan shape originating from the first foot of the plant. Two, three or four branches or shoots of the young plant are chosen to be the ribs of the fan. These shoots are tied to the trellis 8 to 12 inches apart, and trained up the trellis as they grow. The plants are tied securely, but not too tightly, by looping twine underneath the leaf right above a flower/fruit cluster and around the stem. Attach the twine to the horizontal slats of the trellis.

Tomatoes are vigorous vines and send out branches at the base of every leaf where it originates from the stem. These side branches must be nipped each week. If possible, snap these off before they grow 2 inches long; after this a knife is needed to sever them.

Pruning to two to four main branches increases early fruit set lower on the plant and promotes earlier ripening. The first five flower clusters will usually be the ones to produce field-ripened fruit. You can also prune to one main stem and remove all other shoots, but you need more plants for a good yield.

Straw or cut cover crop mulches work well to minimize water splashing, but do cool the soil through shading. A commercial landscape fabric allows water penetration, minimizes splashing and warms the soil, but is made of nonrenewable plastic. The plastic fabric can last many seasons if it's not left out over the winter. To avoid wetting the leaves, use a soaker hose made from recycled tires or a simple drip system.

As a last resort, sulfur sprays are available as a fungus preventative. The spray must be applied every 7 to 14 days. Sulfur is a less toxic fungicide, but it is still toxic and can cause unhealthy side effects.—CE

Worms at Work: Expert Composters

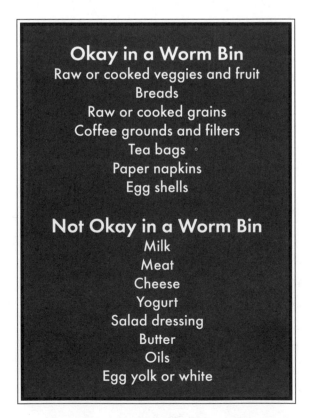

Reduce your household waste and make super rich compost for your garden by composting kitchen scraps in a worm bin. A worm bin is a sturdy box in which worms live and eat organic materials, leaving their castings (manure), which are a nutrient-rich soil amendment for the garden.

The bin is a closed environment filled with a vibrant community of decomposers—red worms, sow bugs, mites, springtails, centipedes, ground beetles and a host of microorganisms—busily working to convert organic wastes into compost. The bedding in the bin provides the habitat for these compost "critters;" your kitchen scraps, buried in the bedding, provide a food source. Here's what you'll need:

A Sturdy Box

- Plywood, heavy-duty plastic, or metal (rodent proof)
- Large enough to handle the material you want to compost (12-18 inches deep)
- The Tilth Worm Bin is 2 feet by 4 feet and handles 8 pounds of food waste per week. Follow the Rule of One: A worm bin can handle 1 pound of food waste per 1 square foot of surface area per 1 week.
- Drainage holes—food wastes are sloppy

Note for apartment dwellers: Make sure a drip pan can be placed underneath the drainage holes.

A Bunch of Moist Bedding

- Bedding is critical; without it you'll have a stinky mess
- Use brown leaves, straw, wood shavings, coconut hulls, sawdust, shredded cardboard or newspaper torn in strips
- Moisten bedding so that it is damp like a wrung-out sponge
- Fill the box to the top!

Add Those Red Wigglers

Eisenia foetida or *Lumbricus rubellus* (red composting worms) enjoy a vegan diet, provide plenty of fresh bedding and the population will triple in a few months. You can buy worms from a Master Composter, through the mail — check gardening and fishing magazines — or call your local solid waste utility for other sources.

Provide a Strict Vegan Diet

- Bury the food waste in a different spot in the bin each time—this allows the worms to consume the material between feedings.
- If your bin smells strongly of rotting food, aerate the bin, add more bedding and reduce the amount of food you bury.
- For odor and fruit fly control, be sure to completely bury all the food waste. Covering the surface of the bedding with a sheet of plastic can also help.

Harvest Your Reward

- When the compost layer fills $2/3$ of the bin, it is time to harvest the finished product.
- Remove $2/3$ of the contents of the bin and incorporate both the compost and worms into your garden bed, then fill the bin with fresh moist bedding and continue composting.
- If the finished compost in the bottom of the bin is very sloppy, add a more absorbent bedding—try coconut hulls or sawdust.
- Winterize your worm bin by filling it with plenty of fresh bedding. In most areas you can keep using the bin all year long.

For more information, see the Resources, page 70.—LT

Okay in a Worm Bin
Raw or cooked veggies and fruit
Breads
Raw or cooked grains
Coffee grounds and filters
Tea bags
Paper napkins
Egg shells

Not Okay in a Worm Bin
Milk
Meat
Cheese
Yogurt
Salad dressing
Butter
Oils
Egg yolk or white

June

July

In the Garden

Anyone who has ever planted a zucchini knows that vegetable raising is fairly easy, it's the harvest that takes time, diligence and commitment. Summer vegetables that are actually fruits will produce more if they are picked two to three times a week. If the fruits of summer squash, cucumbers or beans get too large, the plant begins to die back and yields are reduced.

Although it's tempting to eat that first ripening tomato, if fruits are kept to ripen until they are slightly soft, they not only taste better but they will release a gas that speeds the ripening of other fruit on the vine.

Seed packet descriptions of summer lettuce, spinach, orach and other summer leafy greens frequently define these crops as bolt resistant. When a plant begins to form flowers, it is said to bolt. Bolting significantly changes the flavor of vegetables: lettuce and basil become bitter, spinach tastes acidic and cabbage family plants acquire a sharp sour flavor. Remember, no plant is bolt proof; harvest leafy greens before the plants go to seed. Exceptions include some Asian mustards that are harvested while in flower; these make superb summer brassicas.

To keep summer greens from going to seed early, grow them in fertile soil, keep them watered and pick them frequently. Liquid tea fertilizers provide plants with adequate nitrogen that can help delay flowering.

Fall and winter vegetables started in the heat of summer can be a challenge for busy gardeners. Hot weather causes seed beds to dry out quickly and some seeds, such as lettuce and spinach, will not germinate if the soil is too warm. For a good germination environment in July, it's important to limit water evaporation and reduce soil temperature. Shade cloth is a finely woven mesh material that can be laid over beds or flats to cool the soil. Floating row covers can also be used to help reduce evaporation. Cloche frames can be used as a support for shade cloth or floating row covers.—CE

> ## July
>
> Lakota Elder Black Elk called the July full moon the "Moon when Cherries are Ripe." Generally a dry time, this month is commonly associated with the healing properties and sanctity of water.
>
>

Sow Outdoors

SUMMER VEGETABLES AND HERBS

These summer vegetables will grow in the hot weather of July and August. Keep them watered well to assist in germination and to prevent bolting.

AMARANTH FAMILY *Amaranthaceae*

Amaranth, Greens (Hinn Choy) *A. tricolor and A. lividus:* Bonfire, Coleus Leaf, Mirah, Red Chief, Red Leaf

MUSTARD FAMILY *Brassicaceae*

Oriental Greens: Yu Choi, Bouquet (flowering Green Pac Choi), Hon Tsai Tai (flowering Purple Pac Choi)

BEET FAMILY *Chenopodiaceae*

Lambsquarters: Magentaspreen

Orach: Red

SUNFLOWER FAMILY *Compositae*

Lettuce: Deer Tongue, Esmeralda, Cardinale, Grandpa Admire's, Lobjoit's Green Cos, Loma, Optima, Sierra

PURSLANE FAMILY *Portulacaceae*

Purslane: Goldberger, Garden Large-Leaf

FALL AND WINTER VEGETABLES

For tips on extending the growing season, see "Strategies for Year-Round Gardening" on page 3.

Early July

This is the time to sow the hardiest overwintering root crops and members of the brassica family and root crops. Slower growing winter crops need time to grow before cold weather sets in. Sowing these crops after the middle of the month makes it difficult to reap a good harvest.

CARROT FAMILY *Apiaceae*

Carrots: Shin Kuroda, Kuroda, Fakkel, Bolero, Autumn King, Topweight

Finocchio (bulbing fennel): Zefa Fino

Parsley: Gigante D'Italia, Italian Flat-Leaf

ONION FAMILY *Alliaceae*

Egyptian Walking Onions (Bulbils)

Green Onions: Evergreen White, Ishikuri Long, Red Beard, Welsh Onion, Kincho Long

Pearl Onions: Pacific Pearl

MUSTARD FAMILY *Brassicaceae*

Broccoli, Overwintering: Purple Sprouting, Spring Royalty, White Sprouting

Broccoli, Fall Harvest: Green Valiant, Umpqua, Waltham 29

Cabbage, Portugese: Couve de Tronchuda

Cauliflower: Purple Cape, Walcherin Series, Inca, Nomad, Leamington, Nine-star Perenial, Snow's Winter White

Kale: Siberian, Russian Red (Winter Red), Konserva, Lancito, Morton's Swarm, Redbor

Kale, Ornamental Varieties: Feather Red and White, Coral Queen, Peacock, Christmas Fringed

Radish, European: Black Spanish, Cherry Belle, French Breakfast

Radish, Daikon: Tokinashi, Minowase, Sukurajima Mammoth

Rutabaga: Marian, Laurentian, American Purpletop

Turnips: Orange Jelly, Purple Top White Globe, Golden Ball

Oriental Greens: Pac Choi, Joi Choi, Mei Qing Choi, Kai-laan

SUNFLOWER FAMILY *Compositae*

Escarole: Batavian Full Heart, Cornet d'Anjou

Radicchio: Palla Rossa Especial, Castelfranco, Early Red Trevisio, Giulio

BEET FAMILY *Chenopodiaceae*

Beets: Lutz Greenleaf, Winterkeeper, Chiogga, Yellow Intermediate Mangel

Swiss Chard: Five-Colored Silver Beet (Bright Lights), Charlotte, Fordhook, Rhubarb, Perpetual Spinach

PEA FAMILY *Fabaceae*

(Pea-enation resistant varieties)

Peas, Snap: Cascadia, Sugar Daddy

Peas, Snow: Oregon Giant, Oregon Sugarpod

Late July

Sow the quicker growing crops for fall harvest, and a few chicories that will provide harvest into fall and winter.

MUSTARD FAMILY *Brassicaceae*

Chinese Cabbage: Nerva, Chinese Express, Michihili, Nozaki Early

Collards: Champion, Georgia, Vates, Walking Stick

Kohlrahbi: Vienna, Superschmelz, Rapid

Radish, European: Black Spanish, French Breakfast, Easter Egg, Fluo, Cherry Belle

Radish, Daikon: Tokinashi, Minowase, Sukurajima Mammoth, Rose of China

Turnips: Tokyo Market, Red Milan, Gilfeather, Shogoin

Oriental Greens: Pac Choi, Joi Choi, Mei Qing Choi, Mibu-na

SUNFLOWER FAMILY *Compositae*

Chicory, Catalogna: Dentarella, Puntarella

Chicory, Grumolo: Ceriolo, Lingua di Cane

Endive: Frisee, Perfect, Green Curled, Tres Fine Maraichere

Escarole: Batavian Full Heart, Cornet d'Anjou

Lettuce: Bronze Rodin, Pirat (Brauner Trotzkopf), Little Gem, Brune d'Hiver, Rougette du Midi, Mervielle des Quatre Saisons, Simpson, Brunia

BEET FAMILY *Chenopodiaceae*

Spinach: Nordic, Winter Bloomsdale, Olympia

Flowers to Attract Beneficial Insects

Often gardens are divided: flowers surround the house and line pathways leading to a block of vegetables in a sunny corner. One tenet of organic gardening is to create a diverse plant environment, so go ahead and desegregate your garden. A successful garden includes flowers that benefit vegetable growth.

In their adult stage, many beneficial insects need to sip flower nectar to survive. These insects are attracted to a garden with many flowers and will choose such a place to lay their eggs. After the eggs hatch, the larvae will stay around to get fat on summer insect pests.

The flowers that are most attractive to beneficial insects have open floral nectaries. A flower with open floral nectaries—such as a sunflower—allows small insects to easily access its nectar.

In planning a garden to feed beneficial insects, remember that it's not as important to have lots of flowers in bloom at once as it is to have flowers in bloom as many months of the year as possible. Some of the best flowers for this purpose have a long bloom period.

All members of a plant family share similar flower characteristics, so there are some families that stand out for attracting beneficial bugs:

Sunflower Family *Asteraceae* or *Compositae*

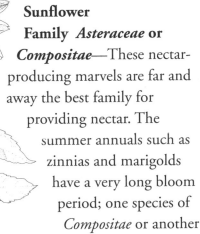

Sunflower

—These nectar-producing marvels are far and away the best family for providing nectar. The summer annuals such as zinnias and marigolds have a very long bloom period; one species of *Compositae* or another is in flower most months of the year. Sunflowers, Jerusalem artichokes and other *Helianthus* spp. also produce a nectar-like substance along their stems, which lady beetles love to eat. Many of the sunflower family plants are cultivars that produce double-, triple- or quadruple-petaled flowers that beneficial insects cannot access. Plant single-petaled varieties for insect attraction.

Mustard

Cabbage Family *Brassicaceae* or *Cruciferae*

—These valuable spring flowering plants provide nectar for lacewings and lady beetles. Some of the best are mustards, crambe, alyssum, cherianthus and arabis.

Carrot Family *Apiaceae* or *Umbelliferae*

—This family is so popular with beneficial insects that sometimes you can't see the flower for the bugs! Members include herbs such as cilantro, dill, lovage and fennel, as well as the attractive flowers of sea holly, thoroughwax and angelicas.

Fennel

Buckwheat Family *Polygonaceae*

—Members of this family primarily bloom in the summer with hundreds of tiny flowers that often attract hover flies and braconid wasps. Annual buckwheat can be grown as a cover crop and turned under after flowering, or try a perennial buckwheat such as *Fagopyrum cymosum*. This plant makes a great stir fry addition when harvested just as it's sprouting.

Buckwheat

Teasel Family

Dipsacaceae—The pincushions are some of the most attractive perennials and annuals for the garden. Adult hover flies spend most of the summer hovering about these flowers.

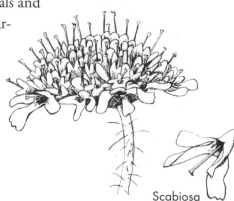

Scabiosa

Pea Family *Fabaceae* or *Leguminosae*—This family does not exclusively supply nectar through its flowers; the vetches have secondary nectaries. These organs are seen as small purple or blue/pink spots on the petioles of the plants, providing food very early in the spring, before most flowers have even considered blooming.

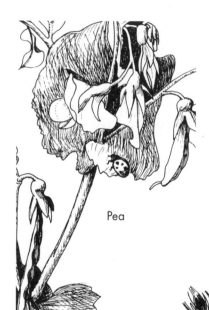

Pea

Pink Family

Caryophyllaceae—The scent of pinks in spring would make anyone envy a bug; sipping all day from these founts of sweetness. The *silenes* (catchflies) are very easy-to-care-for perennials and annuals that also provide nectar.—CE

Pink

Sow Biennial and Perennial Flowers and Herbs

June to early July is often a convenient time to sow biennial and perennial flowers and herbs. The soil temperature is high enough to promote rapid germination and growth without the need for bottom heat or cold frames.

Create a nursery bed. The soil should be moderately fertile but well amended with compost to allow easy transplanting and good water retention. Larger seeded perennials and easy-to-grow biennials start off well in a nursery bed. In the late summer these plants can be transplanted to their permanent homes.

Smaller seeded or slow growing perennials can be sown in flats and pricked out into a nursery bed or pots. Plants in the nursery can be left to overwinter, and in March and April be transplanted to their place in the garden.

The plants in pots can overwinter with some protection. The pots can be sunk into the ground to protect the more tender roots from cold air. Alternately, the pots can be grouped tightly in a cold frame or cloche with sawdust packed 4 to 6 inches thick around the side of the pots. In March and April transplant them into the garden.

ONION FAMILY *Alliaceae*
  Broadleaf Chives *Allium senescens*
  Chives: Grolau, Pink Flowered, Common
  Garlic Chives *Allium tuberosum*
  Welsh Onions *Allium fistulosum*

CARROT FAMILY *Apiaceae*
  Celery Leaved Lovage *Ligusticum apiifolium*
  Fennel *Foeniculum vulgare*
  Garden Angelica *Angelica archangelica*
  Lovage *Ligusticum officinale*
  Masterwort *Angelica atropurpurea*
  Sea Holly *Eryngium amethystinum, E. bourgatii, E. giganteum, E. planum*
  Spring Gold *Lomatium utriculatum*
  Thoroughwax *Bupleurum rotundifolium*

MUSTARD FAMILY *Brassicaceae*
  Cuckoo Flower *Cardamine pratensis*
  Dame's Rocket *Hesperis matronalis*
  Money Plant *Lunaria annua*
  Rockcress *Arabis blepharophylla*
  Sea Kale *Crambe maritima*
  Wallflower *Erysimum* spp. and *Cheiranthus* spp.

PINK FAMILY *Caryophyllaceae*
  Baby's Breath, Perennial *Gypsophylla paniculata*
  Baby's Breath, Creeping *Gypsophylla repens*
  Carnations *Dianthus caryophyllus*
  Cottage Pink *Dianthus plumarius*
  Jove's Flower *Lychnis flos-jovi*
  Maiden Pink *Dianthus deltoides*
  Maltese Cross *Lychnis chalcedonia*
  Rose Campion *Lychnis coronaria*
  Royal Catchfly *Silene regia*
  Sweet William *Dianthus barbatus*

DAISY FAMILY *Compositae*
- Beach Aster *Erigeron glaucus*
- Blanket Flower *Gaillardia pulchella*
- Coneflower *Echinacea* spp.
- Elecampane *Inula helenium*
- Fleabane *Erigeron speciosus*
- Goldenrod *Solidago* spp.
- Mexican Fleabane *Erigeron karvinskianus*
- Michaelmas Daisy *Aster adivaricatus, A. laevis, A. novae-angliae, A. subspicatus,* etc.
- Pyrethrum *Chrysanthemum cinerarifolium*
- Shasta Daisy *Chrysanthemum × superbum*
- Yarrow *Achillea* spp.: Colorado, Summer Pastels, Golden, Pearl
- Woolly Leaf *Eriophyllum lanatum*

TEASEL FAMILY *Dipsacaceae*
- Devil's Bit Scabious *Scabiosa succisa*
- *Knautia macedonica* syn. *Scabiosa rumelica*
- Field Scabious *Knautia arvensis*
- Pincushion Flower *Scabiosa caucasica*
- *Scabiosa ochroleuca*
- Teasel *Dipsacus sylvestris*

PEA FAMILY *Fabaeceae*
- Goat's Rue *Galega bicolor*
- Licorice *Glycyrrhiza glabra*
- Lupine *Lupinus arboreus, L. latifolius, L. polyphyllus* Band of Nobles
- Milk Vetch *Astragalus glycyphyllos*
- Prairie Clover *Petalostemon exile*

MINT FAMILY *Lamiaceae*
- Anise Hyssop *Agastache* spp.: *A. foeniculum, A. mexicana, A. rugosa*
- Bee Balm *Monarda* spp.: *M.menthifolia, M.citrodora, M.didyma*
- Calamintha: Niebita, *C. grandiflora*
- Catmint *Nepeta mussinii*
- Catnip *Nepeta cataria*
- Dragon's Head *Dracocephalum moldavica*
- Lamb's Ears *Stachys lanata*
- Lemon Balm *Melissa officinalis*
- Germander *Teucrium* spp.: *T. hircanicum, T. scoradonia*
- Hyssop *Hyssop officinalis*
- Oregano *Origanum vulgare* var. *hirtum, O. heracleoticum*
- Sages, Culinary *Salvia officinale*
- Sages, Ornamental *Salvia* spp.: *S. argentea, S. pratensis S. sclarea, S.tesquicola, S. translyvanica*
- Thyme *Thymus* spp.: de Provence
- Winter Savory: *Satureja montana*
- Yerba Buena *Satureja douglasii*

LOBELIA FAMILY *Lobeliaceae*
- Cardinal Flower *Lobelia siphilitica*
- *Lobelia × speciosa:* Complexion, Pink Flamingo

MALLOW FAMILY *Malvaceae*
- Hollyhock *Althea rosea*
- Marshmallow *Althea officinalis*
- Mallow *Malva sylvestris*
- Prarie Mallow *Sidalcea candida, Sidalcea malvaeflora*

EVENING PRIMROSE FAMILY *Onagraceae*
- Evening Primrose *Oenothera biennis*
- Mexican Evening Primrose *Oenothera speciosa*
- Sundrops *Oenothera tetragona*
- *Oenothera* spp.: Lemon Sunset, Sunset Boulevard

POPPY FAMILY *Papaveraceae*
- Oriental Poppies *Papaver oriental*
- Icelandic Poppies *Papaver nudicaule*: Champagne Bubbles, Oregon Rainbows
- Welsh Poppies *Meconopsis cambrica*

BUCKWHEAT FAMILY *Polygonaceae*
- Perennial Buckwheat *Fagopyrum cymosum*
- Garden Sorrel *Rumex acetosa*
- Rhubarb: Glaskins Perpetual, Victoria, Champagne Series

BUTTERCUP FAMILY *Ranunculaceae*
- Columbine *Aquiligia* spp.: McKana Giants, *A. atrata, A. chrysantha*
- *Delphinium* spp.: Buttefly hybrids, Magic Fountains
- Monk's Hood *Aconitum* spp.
- Meadow Rue *Thalictrum* spp.

ROSE FAMILY *Rosaceae*
- Alpine Strawberries
- Clove Root *Geum* spp.
- Dropwort *Filipendula vulgaris*
- Salad Burnet *Poterium sanguisorba*

RUE FAMILY *Rutaceae*
- Rue *Ruta graveolens*

FIGWORT FAMILY *Scrophulariaceae*
- Beardtongue *Penstemon* spp. *P. grandiflorus, P. heterophyllus*
- Foxglove *Digitalis* spp.: *D. lanata, D. purpurea* Alba, Heywood
- Mullien *Verbascum* spp.: *V. bombyciferum,* Southern Charm
- Snapdragon *Antirrhinum* spp.
- Veronica spp.:, *V. gentianoides, V. incana, V. spicata*

VALERIAN FAMILY *Valerianaceae*
- Red Valerian *Centranthus ruber*
- Valerian *Valeriana officinalis*

VIOLET FAMILY *Violaceae*
- Black Pansy *Viola nigra*
- Labrador Violet *Viola labradorica*
- Sweet Violet *Viola odorata*: The Czar, Queen Charlotte
- Wild Okra *Viola sororia*
- Winter Pansies *Viola × wittrockiana*: Floral Dance, Universal, Snow Pansies
- Wood violet *Viola riviniana*

August

In the Garden

One bonus of living and gardening in the Maritime Northwest is the possibility of a second spring that sometimes comes with the late summer rains. Fall greens are some of the easiest crops to grow, and will reward the gardener with salads until the first hard frost of November. In a mild year, the greens will last throughout the winter, but wait until September to sow salad to overwinter in a cloche.

Granted, amidst the bounty of the summer harvest and the desire for a vacation, it is hard to contemplate fall vegetables. As incentive, imagine a jade green carpet interwoven with red lettuces and mustards that will be your tasty fall greens.

The cooler weather that takes the heat out of summer frequently arrives during the final two weeks of August. The sun may still shine but its slow descent to the horizon has begun to take the fire out of old Sol. This means that seeds directly sown into the garden will be easier to keep moist than in July and early August. However, compost can help reduce the need for constant watering.

Mix a cover soil for seed with ½ compost and ½ soil, and sift it through a ½-inch mesh screen to remove any large particles. Lightly cover the seeds 2 to 3 times their thickness with the soil and compost mix.

With these tips, you'll be surprised how rewarding and relatively easy to maintain a fall garden can be.—CE

August

In Ireland, Scotland and Wales, Lammas— also called Loaf-mas—was a celebration marked by the making of a loaf of bread from the last of the grain from the previous year. The loaf was shared by the community, and thereafter grain from the new harvest was eaten.

Sow Outdoors

VEGETABLES AND HERBS

Throughout August

Fall greens are a real treat, and a sowing in August will provide a healthy and nutritious harvest.

CARROT FAMILY *Apiaceae*
  Cilantro: Santo
  Chervil: Brussels Winter

ONION FAMILY *Alliacaea*
  Green Onions: Evergreen White, Ishikuri Long, Kincho Long, Red Beard, Winter White Bunching Onion
  Overwintering Onions: Buffalo, Cardinal Red, Walla Walla

MUSTARD FAMILY *Brassicaceae*
  Broccoli Raab: Centoventina, Fall Raab
  Chinese Cabbage: Chinese Express, Nerva
  Cress: Broadleaf, Peppergrass
  Radish: Cherry Belle, Easter Egg, Fluo, French Breakfast, Misato Rose Flesh
  Turnips (for Greens): Gilfeather

BEET FAMILY *Chenopodiaceae*
  Spinach: Nordic, Olympia, Winter Bloomsdale
  Swiss Chard: Five-Colored Silver Beet (Bright Lights), Charlotte, Fordhook, Perpetual Spinach, Rhubarb

SUNFLOWER FAMILY *Compositae*
  Chicory, Catalogna: Dentarella, Puntarella
  Chicory, Gumolo: Ceriolo, Lingua di Cane
  Endive: Frisee, Green Curled, Perfect, Tres Fine Maraichere
  Escarole: Batavian Full Heart, Cornet d'Anjou
  Lettuce: Arctic King, Bronze Rodin, Brune d'Hiver, Little Gem, Merveille des Quatre Saisons, Pirat (Brauner Trotzkopf), Rougette du Midi, Simpson

Late August

The end of August often brings slightly cooler weather, which signals the onset of fall. This provides the perfect conditions for the germination of fall greens and overwintering salad crops that need an early start.

MUSTARD FAMILY *Brassicaceae*
  Arugula
  Cabbage (for spring harvest): First Early Market, Springtime
  Mustards: Giant Red, Green in Snow, Miike Giant, Mizu-na
  Oriental Greens: Tah Tsai, Mibu-na

BEET FAMILY *Chenopodiaceae*
  Spinach: Giant Winter, Skookum, Tyee, Winter Bloomsdale

SUNFLOWER FAMILY *Compositae*
  Shungiku

IRIS FAMILY *Iridaceae*
  Saffron Crocus (from bulbs) *Crocus sativus*

VALERIAN FAMILY *Valerianaceae*
  Corn Salad: Coquille de Louviers, Piedmont, Valgros, Verte d'Etampes, Verte de Cambrai, Vit

PURSLANE FAMILY *Portulacaceae*
  Miner's Lettuce: *Montia perfoliata, Montia sibirica*

Organically Grown Pest Management

Brassica seedlings you are growing now to overwinter, such as kale, cauliflower and broccoli, generally have fewer pest problems than spring-sown plants but are still susceptible to a few. To give an outline of how organic pest management works, I'll go through the process of managing the common cabbage butterfly.

The first step is to know the pest. The adult cabbage butterfly is white to cream in color with one to four dark spots on its wings. This butterfly's flight pattern is very irregular (something only a chaos theorist could attempt to explain), as it flits and darts around the garden. The adults lay small pinhead-sized eggs on the undersides of brassica leaves. The eggs are cream to yellow-orange in color.

Starting off very small and growing to 1 inch in length, it is the caterpillar that does the damage. It is usually green with white markings on its sides (it can be purple in color if feasting on purple cabbage). Dark green frass (caterpillar droppings) and holes in leaves and leaf edges indicate feeding. This pest is primarily a problem for young seedlings and recent transplants. If you have time when the plants are small, crushing the eggs, caterpillars or butterflies is an effective method of control. This is often all backyard gardeners need to do with the help of beneficial insects, which eat the eggs and larvae of the butterfly.

If you have larger plants or many plants, floating row covers are an effective barrier to keep the adults from laying eggs on your plants. Floating row covers also exclude the brassica root maggot, which is active from late July to early September.

If none of these techniques succeed, try a microbial insecticide. *Bacillus thuringiensis* (Bt) is a bacteria that can be applied to plant foliage that caterpillars like to eat. The bacteria invades the intestines of the caterpillar and releases a toxin that slowly kills it. Bt is toxic to all *Lepidoptera* (butterflies and moths), so use it only as a last resort.—CE

Powdery Mildew Prevention and Control

In August, powdery mildew is a common problem for members of the squash family, grapes, roses and other ornamentals. The spores of this fungus invade plant tissue that has dried out due to drought, stress or other damage. It is often seen on a squash plant's oldest leaves, which have dried out just enough to allow this fungal organism to take hold.

The first mildew prevention technique is to grow resistant varieties. Most ornamentals and grapes offer many choices resistant to mildew. As for the squash family members that are eaten as immature fruits (cucumbers, summer squash), sow seeds in succession, removing the older plants as the younger ones come into production. One sowing in April or May followed by another in June works well. Winter squash production is not usually in danger if the plants are growing in fertile conditions.

Soil quality should be the first thing to check if diseases are a problem. Commonly with mildews, the soil is too dry, which causes the leaves to wilt and become susceptible. Ensure that there is adequate calcium, potassium and trace minerals, as these nutrients are important for disease resistance.

Some organic sprays prevent powdery mildew. Garlic works by inhibiting growth and reproduction of the fungus. A stock solution of garlic spray is made by mixing ¼ pound of garlic with 1 quart of water and 1 tablespoon of insecticidal soap spray (found in garden stores) for 5-10 minutes in a blender. Squeeze the liquid through cheese cloth to remove solids. The resulting solution should be diluted 1:10 with water just before spraying. The garlic concentrate will last a month in the refrigerator.

Garlic and soap solutions control powdery mildew on cucumbers and squash: spray weekly after the first blooms. Garlic and soap solutions reduce powdery mildew on grapes as effectively as the more toxic solution, Bordeaux Mix. For grapes, spray them when they bloom, when the leaves emerge and twice during summer new growth. This spray also works as a preventative control of powdery mildews on strawberries and roses.

Cornell University found baking soda, soap and water made an effective preventative of mildew on roses. Mix 1 teaspoon of baking soda and 4 drops of soap spray concentrate in 1 quart of water. This solution must be applied once a week. Compost teas applied twice a month are also an effective preventative measure.

With all homemade mixtures, before spraying the whole plant, always test them on a small portion of the foliage to check for any adverse effects.—CE

When to Water?

If you water your garden at high noon on a summer day, the water is mostly lost to evaporation. Watering in the evening is beneficial for crops that prefer cool weather such as lettuce and spinach. The water cools down the soil after a hot day and helps prevent the plants from bolting prematurely.

Statistically in the Maritime Northwest, most rain falls between the hours of 3 and 6 a.m. Evaporatively speaking, this is also the most efficient time to water, but if you don't like to get up that early, try to water before 10 a.m. This will help reduce evaporation; make the soil darker and able to absorb more heat; and is a good method to use for heat-loving plants like basil, peppers and eggplants.

When watering tomatoes, avoid wetting the leaves, especially with soil that splashes up from under the plant; this soil can transmit late blight (see pg. 43).—CE

Compost Know-How

"At the very base of the organic method lies compost. In its many forms and variations compost is the beautiful substance which gives fertility to soil, productivity to plants and health to man. It is the combination soil conditioner-fertilizer of the organic gardener, and the hub of all his gardening activities. If you are a successful compost maker, chances are 100 to 1 that you are a successful organic gardener."

—Editorial Staff of *Organic Gardening*, Rodale Press, circa. 1960

Composting Yard and Garden Debris

Compost happens—over time any heap of organic matter will become humus. The following information provides the gardener with techniques to make a hot, quickly decomposing compost pile. A compost pile is alive and organic. It needs air, food, water and enough mass to hold heat. A healthy compost pile will grow soil life, which will quickly break down organic matter into rich humus.

AEROBIC VERSUS ANAEROBIC DECOMPOSITION

All organic materials share a common trait: they decompose into rich, soil-like material called compost. Decomposition is nature's way of returning nutrients to the soil so a new generation of organisms can grow. There are two types of decomposition: aerobic and anaerobic. Organic materials that are buried or compacted and deprived of air decompose anaerobically. Anaerobic decomposition is characterized by an ammonia smell, slimy texture and extremely slow conversion to finished compost. A successful compost maker will maintain a pile so that it decomposes aerobically. By turning and fluffing the pile more frequently, a composter adds air, which can provide the ideal conditions for making the building block of the organic garden—compost.

YOUR PILE SHOULD:

- Consist of balanced quantities of carbon (C) and nitrogen (N)
- Be moist like a wrung-out sponge
- Be composed of differently sized pieces—most no bigger than your little finger
- Have a volume of at least 1 cubic yard
- Be aerated so that it is sweet smelling

All organic matter has a carbon to nitrogen ratio that determines how slowly or quickly it will break down. All plant material is carbon-based; "greens" have a lower C:N ratio, and "browns" have a higher C:N ratio. Greens break down faster than browns.

C:N ratios for some common materials

Material	Ratio	Category
food scraps	15:1	GREENS
grass clippings	19:1	GREENS
rotted manure	25:1	GREENS
combined mix	30:1	IDEAL
corn stalks	60:1	BROWNS
leaves	40-80:1	BROWNS
straw	80:1	BROWNS
paper	170:1	BROWNS
sawdust, wood chips	500:1	BROWNS

For fast, hot composting, mix brown and green materials to achieve a 30:1 ratio of carbon:nitrogen. One way to achieve the correct C:N ratio is to mix half deciduous leaves or straw with half green herbaceous plants or grass clippings. Assemble your materials, mixing them well (as if you were tossing a salad) and adding water until all of the materials are moist like a wrung-out sponge. For the best quality, add some soil. For sweet smelling, aerobic compost, avoid over watering, and aerate by turning the pile every 7-10 days; a well-tended pile will be ready in 2-3 months.

For slow, cold composting, place dampened organic matter in a pile (or bin) and wait. In 12-18 months it

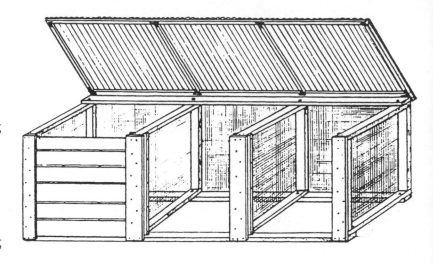

will be composted and ready to use in your garden. Kitchen or food scraps can attract rodents, and are best used in worm bins or other food waste systems.

 A bin is not necessary, but makes managing the material much easier. A bin that has three fixed sides and a removable front is ideal for turning.

 Many manufactured bins are meant to be holding bins for slow, cold composting—making turning your compost a bit of an ordeal.

 Your compost system (or area) should have a place to store materials, a place to mix and pile materials and a place to keep finished compost until you are ready for it in the garden.

STICK YOUR HAND IN IT

To determine how your compost pile is progressing, you need to examine it. How it looks, feels and smells tells you what the pile needs to compost most efficiently.

 If your pile smells like ammonia or rotten eggs, your pile may have too much moisture, too many "greens" and not enough air. Solution: Turn the pile and add "brown" materials such as leaves or straw.

 If your freshly made pile is damp and sweet smelling but will not heat up, you may not have enough nitrogen. Solution: Add fresh "greens" or a nitrogen fertilizer. Note: Your compost may be finished if it looks like rich, dark soil.

 If your pile is dry and doesn't seem to be doing anything, you may not have enough moisture and may have too much woody material. Solution: Turn and water the pile, add fresh "greens" or nitrogen fertilizer, and chop or shred woody materials.

 If your pile is too hot to touch (over 150° F), you may have too much green material and are burning off many of the nutrients in the compost. Solution: Add more brown materials or more water to cool the pile down.

 If your pile looks like a brush heap, you may have

included too many large materials. Solution: Shred or chop woody material, water thoroughly and add "greens" or nitrogen fertilizer.

 If your pile is moist and warm in the middle but cold around the edges, your pile is too small. Solution: Add more materials to create a volume of 1 cubic yard and moisten.

For more information and ready-made compost sources, see the Resources section on page 70.—LT

Okay in Your Compost Pile

grass
deciduous leaves
plants
annual weeds
house plants
flowers
twigs the size of your little finger
chopped hedge prunings

Not Okay in Your Compost Pile

kitchen scraps
evergreens
branches bigger than your little finger
invasive weeds (morning glory, ivy,
quack grass, buttercup, blackberry)
noxious weeds
diseased plants
dog and cat feces
weed seeds
poisonous plants

September

In the Garden

September is a busy month in Maritime Northwest gardens. The whole look and feel of the garden can change over the course of one short month. Overwintering cover crops can be sown to provide nutrients and organic matter for next year's garden. Sowing salad greens from late September into the first weeks of October is important because small plants (1 or 2 inches tall) overwinter better than larger plants. Overwintering plants have unique soil fertility needs to help them survive the cold and thrive come spring. Excessive nitrogen produces fast growth full of water, so don't provide too much nitrogen because this will make plants more susceptible to frost damage. The goal is balanced growth throughout the fall and early winter, then in the spring, add top dressings of high-nitrogen organic fertilizers or composted manure to spur faster spring growth.

In an established garden, the nutrients necessary for fall plant establishment can be supplied by cover crops and compost. Incorporate well-rotted compost into the entire garden bed. The comparatively warm soil temperatures of fall allow soil bacteria to mineralize the nutrients in the compost, making them available to winter vegetables.

Summer cover crops provide additional fertility for overwintering vegetables. Two to three weeks before transplanting or sowing into beds, turn under cover crops or chop them with a hoe. Keep the beds moist to facilitate cover crop decomposition and to pre-germinate weed seeds. After weeds sprout, chop them into the soil before planting your crop.

The process of double digging, or preparing the soil to 18-24 inches deep, allows roots good penetration and better access to nutrients. Permanent beds and pathways help keep you from compacting the soil with your feet, which can damage the soil in the wet winter months.

Thin your plants a little more than you would in the spring (up to twice as far apart). The increased distance between plants improves air circulation when plants are grown in cloches and reduces root competition for nutrients. Thinning also provides baby vegetables for munching.—CE

September

The ancient Incans celebrated the Feast of the Moon this month with dancing and feasting. This is also the birth month of Quetzalcoatl, "the Feathered Serpent" god known in Mexico for teaching people cultivation and the use of metals.

Sow Outdoors

VEGETABLES

Early September

Sow greens that need to be protected under a cloche to allow for harvest throughout the winter. The variable weather will greatly affect the amount a gardener will harvest from this sowing, but most years you will be surprised by how hardy these plants can be.

CARROT FAMILY *Apiaceae*
- **Cilantro:** Santo
- **Chervil:** Brussels Winter

MUSTARD FAMILY *Brassicaceae*
- **Arugula**
- **Cabbage** (for spring harvest): First Early Market, Springtime
- **Cress:** Broadleaf, Landcress
- **Mustard:** Gai Choi, Giant Red, Green in Snow, Green Wave, Mizuna
- **Radish:** Misato Rose Flesh

BEET FAMILY *Chenopodiaceae*
- **Spinach:** Winter Bloomsdale, Giant Winter, Skookum, Tyee

SUNFLOWER FAMILY *Compositae*
- **Endive:** Frisee, Green Curled, Perfect, Tres Fine Maraichere (These are sometimes damaged by cold winters under a cloche, but sometimes not; go ahead and try.)
- **Lettuce:** Bronze Rodin, Brune D'Hiver, Little Gem, Perella Red and Green, Rougette du Midi, Ruben's Red, Winter Density

Late September (all overwintering)

These crops are meant to overwinter. The seedlings should go through the winter with just four to eight true leaves. In late winter and early spring, the plants have a growth spurt, providing large harvests in February or March when most gardeners are just getting started. Generally, this sowing does not need a cloche to overwinter, but in years with cold weather and no snow cover, some damage can occur without a cloche.

CARROT FAMILY *Apiaceae*
- **Caraway**
- **Carrot:** Merida
- **Chervil:** Brussels Winter
- **Sweet Cicely**

GRASS FAMILY *Gramineae*
- **Overwintering Grains:** Barley, Rye, Spelt, Triticale, Wheat

MUSTARD FAMILY *Brassicaceae*
- **Arugula**
- **Arugula, Rustic** *Arugula sylvatica*
- **Mustard:** Green in Snow, Green Wave, Mizu-na

Radish: Misato Rose Flesh

PEA FAMILY *Fabaceae*
- **Peas, Snow:** Chinese Snow
- **Fava Beans:** Aprovecho Select, Aquadulce, Banner, Sweet Lorane

BEET FAMILY *Chenopodiaceae*
- **Beets:** Chioggia, Lutz Green Leaf, Winterkeeper, Yellow Intermediate Mangel
- **Spinach:** Winter Bloomsdale, Giant Winter, Tyee

SUNFLOWER FAMILY *Compositae*
- **Lettuce:** Brune d'Hiver, Perella, Red Tinged Winter, Ruben's Red Romaine, Winter Density, Winter Marvel

PEA FAMILY *Fabaceae*
- Peas, Snow: Chinese Snow

GRASS FAMILY *Gramineae*
- **Overwintering Grains:** Barley , Rye, Spelt, Triticale, Wheat

FLOWERS

Hardy Annuals

Hardy annuals are the organic gardener's best friend (until they go to seed, when they may be your worst nightmare). Be that as it may, sown with discretion, hardy annuals fill a useful niche in the garden. Nature abhors a vacuum, and most gardens are filled with soil vacuums that she attempts to fill with weeds. The truth is that bare soil will grow plants, so why not fill that bare soil with flowering plants? Hardy annuals can be thugs—wantonly casting their seeds about or growing too tall and smothering less rambunctious plant life. This hardy annual flower list is divided into large annuals good for standing on their own or mixed in with large plants, and smaller hardy annuals useful for weed suppression and to knit in with growing perennials or shrubs.

SHORT

Alyssum *Lobularia maritima*
California Poppy *Eschscholzia* spp.: *E. californica* var. *maritima, E. caespitosa*, Moonglow, Milkmaid, Inferno
California Bluebells *Phacelia* spp.: *P. campanularia, P. parryi*, Tropical Surf
Baby Blue Eyes *Nemophila menziesii*
Papaver commutatum
Farewell-to-Spring *Clarkia* spp.: *C. amoena, C. bottea, C. rubicunda, C. unguiculata*
Fried Eggs *Limnanthes douglasii*
Johnny Jump Ups *Viola tricolor*
Lupines, Annual *Lupinus nanus, L. densiflorus*
Mountain Phlox *Linanthus grandiflorus*
Rose Angel *Silene coeli-rosa*

TALL

Bachelor's Buttons *Centaurea cyanus*
Breadseed Poppy *Papaver somniferum*
Corn Cockle *Agrostemma githago*: Milas
Forget-Me-Nots *Myosotis sylvatica*
Larkspur *Delphinium ajacis*: Frosted Skies, Imperial Strain
Love-in-a-Mist *Nigella* spp.: Curiosity, Persian Jewels
Peony Flowered Poppy *Papaver paeoniflorum*: Black Peony, Golden Peony
Shirley Poppies *Papaver rhoeas*: Mother of Pearl, Angel Wings
Sweet Peas *Lathyrus odoratus*: Cupani, Royal Mix, Old Spice
Toad Flax *Linaria maroccana*

Tilth Organic
Harvest Fair

Bring your friends and family to celebrate the harvest!

The Seattle Tilth Organic Harvest Fair offers the best organic produce money can buy and more of Washington state's organic farmers together in one place than you can meet anywhere else.

The Fair (which occurs in early September) also features a children's garden fair, cooking and gardening demonstrations, live music, and organic lunch vendors.

Soil Testing

Gardeners and garden writers often neglect soil tests. This is due either to a lack of interest or to the belief that very few nutrients are available in Maritime Northwest soils, so all nutrients should be added.

Granted, when starting a garden from scratch, most gardeners don't have much to work with. Our modern culture treats soil like dirt. For new gardens, a soil test provides a base line to use in comparison with future test results. And for a mature garden, a soil test can pinpoint micronutrient deficiencies and provide very useful information about the effects of your cultural practices on the soil. September is a good time to do a soil test and add the necessary lime or other rock minerals that take a long time to become part of the living soil.

The soil test companies listed below provide different levels of service and detailed advice. Most will provide information on interpreting the test data.

The Basic:
U. Mass Soil Test Lab
West Experiment Station
N. Pleasant St.
University of Massachusetts
Amherst, MA 01003

1 cup soil; $7; two-week turn around; tests Lead, Cadmium, Nitrogen, Phosphorus, Potassium and pH; additional $3 covers organic matter. Write for directions on how to do a soil test. No phone calls, please.

The Deluxe:
A&L Western Agricultural Labs
10220 S.W. Nimbus Ave., Bldg. K-9
Portland, OR 97223
(503) 968-9225
For $30: organic matter, Nitrogen, Phosphorus, Potassium, Calcium, Magnesium and pH with buffer index, base saturation rate for mineral salts.
For $80: all of the above, plus NO3, S, Zn, Mn, Fe, Cu, B and salinity.

The Supreme:
(Woods End Research)
Box 297
Mount Vernon, ME 04352
(207) 293-2457   E-mail: info@woodsend.org
Includes what's tested for "the deluxe" plus soil aggregate quality; biological activity and nutrient turnover; soil respiration; and compost and soil amendment maturity. Contact them for prices and garden group discounts.—CE

Recognizing Nutrient Deficiencies in Plants

An observant gardener can recognize symptoms of nutrient deficiencies as they appear; your concerns can be dismissed or affirmed by a quality soil test. Macronutrient deficiency symptoms are the easiest to detect.

Nitrogen—Too little nitrogen is marked by pale yellow leaves and leaf veins, and early drop of older leaves with contrasting healthy-looking growing tips. Once plants begin to fruit, slight nitrogen deficiency symptoms are common and not harmful, unless growth and fruiting are obviously stunted.

Phosphorus—Purplish leaves and stems, pale new leaves with yellow margins, and poor flowering and fruiting indicate phosphorus deficiency. Temporary symptoms are common in the late spring when cold, wet conditions make soil phosphorus unavailable.

Potassium—Scorched leaf margins, mottled yellowing of older leaves, weak stems and reduced disease resistance mark too little potassium. Harvests from these plants do not keep well. Deficiencies can be caused by excessive amending with dolomite lime.

Calcium—Calcium deficiency can cause flower buds to be poorly formed or to drop off, leaf curl, poor root formation, poor fungal disease resistance, and mottled leaves on beets and other *Chenopodiaceae*. Tomatoes and peppers may have blossom-end rot. Calcium deficiencies are very common in Maritime Northwest soils.

Sulfur—Marked by pale or yellow new growth, sulfur deficiency is usually only a problem in new gardens with low organic matter, or in gardens that are consistently over watered; sulfur is easily leached from the soil.

Magnesium—Low magnesium is indicated by yellow leaves with green leaf veins and unexpected bronze foliage spots, or very weak and brittle twigs on woody plants. This is usually a problem only in new gardens.—CE

Rights for Farm Workers Equals Safer Food for All

Most produce we buy at local groceries has passed through the hands of a farm worker. Farm workers are an integral part of the agricultural production of this country and yet they experience very difficult working conditions, low pay and unhealthy housing for themselves and their families. When pesticides are sprayed, farm workers are on the front lines and are the most frequently exposed and most at risk.

Agricultural workers are excluded from many of the basic rights guaranteed to other workers and are in a vulnerable position that discourages them from reporting unsafe or unhealthy conditions. We as consumers can improve the lives of farm workers and promote a safer food supply by supporting farm workers' rights such as the right to collectively bargain with their employers. When workers are not afraid to speak up in the workplace then they can seek enforcement of laws and regulations for proper field sanitation, as well as report environmental conditions on farms, such as how pesticides are used. When farm workers have these basic rights, the products consumers buy in stores will be of better quality and the whole food system safer and more equitable.

Talk to the produce manager in your store and encourage them to buy from farmers and distributors who support the rights of farm workers. Support United Farm Workers (UFW) campaigns in Washington state by calling the UFW in Seattle at (206) 443-7645. In Oregon, contact *Pineros y Campesinos Unidos del Noroeste* (PCUN), the Oregon Farm Workers Union at (503) 982-1031.—JJ

October

In the Garden

October is the month to prepare cloches for winter. The weather can still be quite pleasant, but you can feel the cold coming on in your bones. Cloches are the best protective covering to overwinter most greens. The Maritime Northwest usually experiences diffuse light through heavy cloud cover during the winter; cloches allow this light to enter from all directions. In a cold frame with solid sides, the edges are often shaded resulting in less area to produce healthy plants.

Venting a cloche allows for more air flow across the surface of plants, which is important for disease prevention. Don't keep cloches closed all fall and winter long; instead, open the ends of the cloche on days above 40° F. The soil under a cloche can get quite dry, so if the weather is mild and rainy, remove the plastic skin over the cloche to wet the soil. This probably needs to be done twice a month, and more often as the weather warms in the spring.

Cover crops can still be sown in beds where plants have been removed. As October progresses, the best cover crops to sow are Austrian field peas and fava beans, with any grain as a support. These germinate in cold soils better than other cover crops. Place an older piece of floating row cover over the soil to discourage birds, as they can quickly consume a recently sown cover crop. Remember to weight the edges and remove the cover after the seed has germinated.—CE

October

The end of this month is reserved for honoring the dead by many cultures around the world. Our gardens now begin to show us what was believed by the ancient Druids to be the closing of the natural circle of the year.

Sow Outdoors

Throughout October

If you like to eat onions, garlic and other fragrant alliums this is the month to get them planted. You can sow favas now so you can enjoy fresh favas simmering in green garlic in April and May. This is also the month to plant flower bulbs.

VEGETABLES AND HERBS

ONION FAMILY *Alliaceae*

Garlic, Silverskin: California Late, Gilroy, Italian Early, Nichols, Nootka Rose, Polish White, Rose du Var, Silver Rose

Garlic, Artichoke: Asian Tempest, Burgundy, Inchelium Rakkyo, , Red Garlic, Rocambole: Chet's Spanish Roja

Allium chinense (**Jiao tou**)

Shallots: Atlantic, Dutch Yellow, Frog's Legs (Pear), Gray French, Jersey

Multiplier Onions: Red, Yellow

PEA FAMILY *Fabaceae*

Peas, Snow: Chinese Snow

Fava Beans: Aprovecho Select, Aquadulce, Banner, Sweet Lorane

GRASS FAMILY *Gramineae*

Overwintering Grains: Barley , Rye, Spelt, Triticale, Wheat

FLOWERS

Spring Blooming Bulbs

The nursery bulb industry seems to exist to sell bulbs that act as annuals; the plants never perform in subsequent years quite as well as they do that first year. Here is a short list of bulbs and varieties that will naturalize and increase in splendor year after year, if given proper care.

Anemone blanda: Charmer, Violet Star, White Splendor

Brodiaea spp.

Crocus spp.: *C. tommasinianus, C. chrysanthus:* Ladykiller, Blue Bird, Snowbunting

Daffodils: Arctic Gold, Ceylon, Misty Glen, Tahiti, Jetfire, Quail, Thalia, Plenus, Bell Song

Dog's Tooth Violet *Erythronium* spp.: *E. dens-canis, E. revolutum,* Pagoda

Fritillaria spp.: Checker Lily, Crown Imperial

Glory of the Snow *Chionodoxa* spp.: *C. forbesii, C. luciliae*

Grape Hyacinth *Muscari* spp.: *M. armeniacum , M. latifolium*

Iris reticulata: Joyce, Natascha, J.S. Dijt, Edward

Lily *Lilium* spp.: *L. henryi, L. pardalinum, L. regale,* Oriental hybrids, Trumpet hybrids

Onions, Ornamental *Allium* spp.: *A. christophii, A. cowanii, A. moly, A. sphaerocephalum*

Snowflakes *Leucojum* spp. and *Galanthus* spp.

Tulipa spp.: *Cultivars of T. fosteriana, T. greiggi, T. kaufmanniana, T. batalinii,* Darwin hybrids

Trillium spp.

Legumes for Fixing Nitrogen

Growing legume cover crops is one of the most important tools for increasing soil fertility in an organic garden. Legumes (peas, vetches, clovers, beans and others) grow in a symbiotic relationship with soil-dwelling bacteria. The bacteria take gaseous nitrogen from the air in the soil and feed this nitrogen to the legumes; in exchange the plant provides carbohydrates to the bacteria. This is why legume cover crops are said to "fix" or provide a certain amount of nitrogen when they are turned under for the next crop or used for compost.

Rhizobacteria are naturally present in the soil, but their populations are often too low to maximize nitrogen fixation. For the best nitrogen fixation, inoculate or coat the seed with purchased rhizobium. Specific strains of rhizobacteria work with different legumes. Read the packages carefully to ensure that you purchase the correct rhizobacteria for the legume cover crop you have chosen to sow.

To coat the seed, put it in a container and moisten it slightly with water or milk. The liquid will help the inoculant coat the seed. Sprinkle approximately 1 heaping tablespoon of inoculant per $\frac{1}{2}$ pound of seed.

The rhizobia are living organisms, so you should sow the seed as soon as possible after coating it. Do not leave inoculated seed in the sun because the soil-dwelling creatures can't live in UV light.

All legumes need adequate supplies of phosphorus, calcium and sulfur. Fall is a good time to test the soil for these major nutrients and adjust the soil content by adding lime, rock phosphate or gypsum as needed.—CE

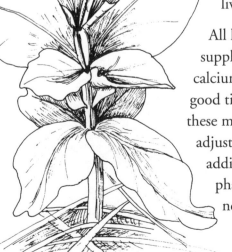

Fava bean

Annual Winter Cover Crops Chart

TYPE OF COVER CROP	SOWING RATE (# OF SEED PER 1000 SQ. FEET)	# OF NITROGEN FIXED	NOTES
Austrian Field Peas *Pisum arvense*	2 to 4	70 to 120 per acre	Can be sown as late as November; easy to sow and incorporate into the soil; matures in May if sown in October.
Magnus Field Peas *Pisum arvense*	2 to 4	70 to 120 per acre	High biomass production; matures earlier than other cover crops; ready to turn under in late April.
Crimson Clover *Trifolium incarnatum*	1/2 to 2	80 to 90 per acre	Easiest cover crop to turn into the soil; ready in early May with spectacular flaming crimson blossoms. Great for undersowing existing crops; does not fix much nitrogen in fertile soils.
Bell Beans/Fava Beans *Vicia faba*	2 to 4	80 to 120 per acre	Has a strong taproot that breaks up heavy or compacted soils and leaves a lot of organic matter in the soil. These vetch relatives can grow as high as 3 to 5 feet making this plant a bit difficult to incorporate into the garden. Tasty edible flowers are an added bonus.
Lana Vetch *Vicia dasycarpa*	1 to 3	200 to 275 per acre	Introduced by the USDA, this vetch fixes the most nitrogen per acre of any annual; has strong spring growth and matures in late May. Fully hardy to 10° F. Sow with a small grain to support its vining growth. All vetches are the best cover crops to assist in creating a good soil structure or tilth.
Common Vetch *Vicia sativa*	1 to 3	175 to 225 per acre	Hardy (to 0° F) and cheap to boot makes this vetch an all-purpose choice. Like all vetches, the plant has secondary floral nectaries (located at the base of leaf stalks), which are an important nectar source for beneficial insects in the early spring. Sow with a small grain to support its vining growth; harvest in early May.

SMALL GRAINS TO SOW WITH LEGUMES FOR SUPPORT AND GOOD SOIL COVERAGE

Mix grains with legumes seed, 85 percent legume and 15 percent grain, for maximum nitrogen fixation and adequate vine support.

Cereal Rye
Secale cereale
Good winter growth under cool conditions, prolific biomass production and tall plants capable of supporting vining growth make rye the best small grain cover crop to grow with vetches. Ready to harvest in early May. (Note: Do not confuse this plant with rye grass that is short, does not produce much biomass and is hard to kill by digging under.)

Winter Wheat
Triticum aestivum
Commonly offered in seed catalogs, bread wheat provides an extensive fibrous root system that assists in developing soil tilth and adds organic matter to the soil. Ready to till under or harvest in April or May, it grows well with vetches.

Spelt
Triticum spelta
Spelt's value lies in its ability to grow very well in a Maritime Northwest climate that has excessively moist winters and springs. The plant puts on more biomass than wheat and rarely lodges or falls over in rich garden soils—as rye and wheat sometimes do.

Barley
Hordeum vulgare
Barley becomes ready to harvest as a cover crop before other grains, so it is useful to mix with peas as support for tilling under in early March.

NON-LEGUME COVER CROPS FOR BUILDING ORGANIC MATTER AND NUTRIENT RECYCLING

Cover crops that do not fix nitrogen also have a role to play in the vegetable garden. These crops protect the soil from the impact of excessive rainfall and tap nutrients that have leached out of the root zone of crop plants. The result is a recycling of important nutrients back to the biologically rich top layer of the soil, as well as adding organic matter to the soil by increasing carbon reserves. Most of these cover crops are sown in late August or early September because they mature faster in spring than the legumes. They can be harvested or turned under in February or March before planting the early spring garden.

CROP	OUNCES PER 100 SQUARE FEET	NOTES
Mustard *Brassica juncea*	1	A deep-rooted cover crop that can accumulate calcium, sulfur and potassium from the subsoil and bring them to the topsoil in an organic form, this broadleaf plant covers the soil quickly and smothers overwintering weeds. It is a superb cover crop to plant before spring peas or root crops, and is ready to harvest in February or March.
Rape *Brassica napus*	1	Similar properties as the above plant, this one has a deeper and larger tap root that assists in loosening and creating good tilth in heavy soils.
Arugula *Eruca sativa*	1	Not commonly offered as a cover crop, but it grows like a weed while smothering other weeds, puts on lots of biomass and is tasty to boot.
Corn Salad *Valerianella locusta*	1	Corn salad is very cold resistant, but must be started in late August to achieve good growth before winter sets in for real. It blooms and is ready to dig under in March, and it breaks down quickly in the soil. It does not compete well in very weedy beds.

Why Add Lime to the Soil?

Water-soluble nutrients are most available to plants when the soil pH is slightly acid—a pH reading of 6.3 to 6.8. Most Maritime Northwest soils have high acidity (low pH) due to excessive rainfall, which causes positively charged minerals, calcium and magnesium in particular to leach out of the soil. Calcium also helps soil microorganisms function, especially the nitrogen-fixing rhizobia associated with some cover crops. Magnesium is the key element in creating chlorophyll.

Calcium and magnesium need to be in balance in the soil. A good ratio is 1 part magnesium to 5 parts calcium (1:5). This ratio can be radically thrown off by applications of dolomite lime year after year. This is a common problem for backyard gardeners, because dolomite is usually the only limestone available at garden centers.

As a general rule, add dolomite lime once in four years, and add agricultural limestone the other three years. By providing lime to the soil you can neutralize the pH by replenishing positively charged mineral nutrients that are necessary for plant growth. The calcium and magnesium in lime are vital plant macronutrients. Calcium builds plant tissue and assists them in fighting disease organisms. Making generalizations about the amount of lime necessary to change soil pH is risky because it depends on your specific soil makeup, so a soil test is indispensable. Heavy clay soils need much more lime to change

pH than sandy soils do. Also, as the pH reaches 6.0 and above, less lime is needed to make a dramatic change. However, WSU Cooperative extension does recommend applying 3 pounds of lime for sandy soils and 5-6 pounds of lime for clay soils every 2 years.

Sources for calcium, sulfur, magnesium and pH adjustment:

Agricultural Limestone: 94 percent Calcium Carbonate—Very pure calcium carbonate should be used when calcium and pH adjustment are needed but no magnesium is wanted. It is hard to find outside of mail-order catalogs, but necessary for Maritime Northwest gardens.

Dolomite Limestone: 50 percent Calcium Carbonate, 40 percent Magnesium Carbonate—The most commonly available form of limestone, it has a substantial amount of magnesium and should not be used if a soil test determines sufficient levels of magnesium.

Gypsum: 98 percent Calcium Sulfate—Used to supply calcium and sulfur without changing soil pH; combined with compost gypsum helps to improve the soil structure of heavy clay soils.

Oyster Shell Lime: 36 percent Calcium Carbonate and Trace Minerals—A by-product of the seafood industry, oyster shells are finely ground to allow easy soil incorporation. Oyster shell lime must be applied for a number of years to fully change pH and provide adequate calcium.—CE

Organic Wine Tasting

Support the growing organic wine industry by attending Tilth's annual Organic Wine Tasting!

~

Begun in 1998, it is held in Seattle in late October or early November and offers wines from around the world, including excellent products from Washington vintners.

~

Tastings are accompanied by great food made by Seattle chefs with local produce, plus there is music and the opportunity to learn about growing grapes organically.

November

In the Garden

If you aren't careful this month, you could end up chasing all kinds of debris around the garden. The winds begin to blow and nature shows her wild side by creating chaos out of ordered gardens. When they're not swirling around, gather leaves from lawns or paved areas to use as mulch in the garden. If you're not growing cover crops in spring vegetable beds, mulch them with 3 to 5 inches of leaves. This will protect the soil from excessive rainfall and increase earthworm activity. Before planting in the spring rake away undecomposed leaves to make compost or leaf mold.

Leaves also can be used as a mulch for winter root crops. Mulch 4 to 6 inches deep to make the crops easier to dig and to protect them from hard frosts. In rural areas, mice can be a problem by eating vegetables under the mulch. If this is your case, store your roots inside in moist sand in a room separated from stored fruits. As they ripen, stored apples and pears in particular release a gas that promotes ripening and will cause root crops to rot.

Don't be too tidy. Plants that naturally grow under trees can handle autumn leaves—in fact, they like it. Brush the leaves off the crowns of plants and lightly toss them between plants. A leaf mulch protects roots from heavy frosts. Many gardeners claim that raking leaves controls slugs and root weevils. However, significant evidence suggests that raking leaves increases the populations of these pests by eliminating the hiding places of predatory beetles. These beetles need cover, and mulch protects them from hungry birds and cold. Rotting logs and piles of stones are also excellent winter hiding places for beneficial insects.—CE

November

Give thanks for your garden's bounty at Thanksgiving time by eating foods that you have grown or would like to grow next year: parsnips, cabbage, cauliflower, parsley and corn salad to name a few.

Sow Outdoors

VEGETABLES AND HERBS

Early November

Garlic and fava beans can still be sown. The garlic often does not sprout until January or February, but the roots are actively growing. Good garlic production relies on a well-established root structure to support healthy leaf growth in the spring.

ONION FAMILY *Alliaceae*

Garlic, Silverskin: Silver Rose, Polish White, California Late, Italian Early, Nootka Rose, Gilroy, Nichols, Rose du Var

Garlic, Artichoke: Asian Tempest, Inchelium Red, Purple Cauldron, Chamiskuri

Garlic, Hardneck: Burgundy, Spanish Roja

PEA FAMILY *Fabaceae*

Fava Beans: Aprovecho Select, Sweet Lorane, Aquadulce, Banner

FLOWERS

Anemone blanda: Charmer, Violet Star, White Splendor

Brodiaea spp.

Crocus spp.: *C. tommasinianus, C. chrysanthus:* Ladykiller, Blue Bird, Snowbunting

Daffodils: Arctic Gold, Bell Song, Ceylon, Jetfire, Misty Glen, Plenus, Quail, Thalia, Tahiti

Dog's Tooth Violet *Erythronium* spp.: *E. dens -canis, E. revolutum,* Pagoda

Fritillaria spp.: Checker Lily, Crown Imperial

Glory of the Snow *Chionodoxa* spp.: *C. forbesii, C. luciliae*

Iris reticulata: Joyce, Natascha, J.S. Dijt, Edward

Onions, Ornamental *Allium* spp.: *A. christophii, A. cowanii, A. moly, A. sphaerocephalum*

Spring Snowflakes *Leucojum* spp. and *Galanthus* spp.

Tulip spp.: Cultivars of *T. fosteriana, T. greiggi, T. kaufmanniana,* Darwin Hybrids

Trillium spp.

Leaf Mold: Worth the Wait

Before the age of soil-less, peat-based potting soils, composted leaves (called leaf mold) were a key component of the best potting soils. In some areas of the country, gardeners can still buy leaf mold in bags. This material is not hard to make, but it takes time and patience. A leaf-only compost pile can take up to two years to decompose into humus suitable for potting soil.

The carbon to nitrogen ratio in most leaves (40-80 parts carbon to 1 part nitrogen) is why this composting process takes so much time. Some gardeners are tempted to add a nitrogen source to a leaf compost pile, but there are some drawbacks to adding other products to pure leaves. Blood meal, fish meal and the like are sometimes used as nitrogen sources in compost. If added to a leaf pile, these result in a product that may be too rich in nitrogen for potting soils. Too much nitrogen promotes leggy seedling growth and can cause an increase in insect damage and diseases. Pure leaf mold has a coarse, crumb-like structure that is an excellent addition to potting soils because it increases air content.

Tree leaves are the best concentrators of calcium, magnesium and trace minerals on the terrestrial world. These minerals are very important to seedling growth, and by composting the leaves, these nutrients are made easily available to young plants. All leaves are not created equal; common leaves in order of best mineral content are: oak, beech, maple, ash and alder.

So, stockpile leaves today for future rewards. Leaves can be stored in a simple bin constructed of a 3-foot-wide piece of hog wire bent to make a cylinder and stood up on end. The ends of the wire can then be secured to each other to allow the bin to stand. It is beneficial to shade or cover the leaf mold pile during the summer to keep it from drying out.

Leaves from the walnut family and horse chestnut trees should be left under the tree or sent away to compost because these trees concentrate chemicals in their leaves that can inhibit the germination and growth of many plants.—CE

November

Club-Root of Brassicas
Plasmodiophora brassicae

Members of the mustard or brassica family (including the cultivated cabbage, broccoli, cauliflower, kale, collards, mustards, turnips, radishes and the weed shepherd's purse) are host to a fungus-like slime mold that causes the plants to develop swollen and malformed roots resembling a club. Hence the apt, common name club-root.

Infected plants commonly wilt at midday and slightly recover the next morning. The plants are stunted and the harvestable yield of the plant, be it root, leaves or flower heads, is severely reduced or nonexistent.

Control measures for any disease should be based on the real cause of the problem, not merely an attempt to mask the symptoms of the disease. Therefore, in order to reasonably control club-root, one must consider its life history. Also, to effectively control club-root, a gardener must practice not one, but all of the cultural techniques outlined here.

The essential facts to consider are: (1) The disease organism is perpetuated by means of resting spores imbedded in the root tissue of the plant. (2) These spores are liberated into the soil upon disintegration of the large roots and crown of the plant. (3) The spores remain dormant in the soil for three to five years. (4) The virulence of the organism is favored by acid soils. (5) The organism is favored by soils with high moisture content. (6) The organism lives on weed hosts belonging to the mustard family.

The first step in reducing club-root is to completely remove the root of any diseased brassica at harvest. Designate a plastic compost bin as a brassica isolation tank; the compost from this bin should not be used on any vegetable production bed. Alternately, the affected brassicas could be sent to the landfill.

Reduce the number of brassicas grown in the garden. In the Maritime Northwest, brassicas can be grown every month of the year, tempting the gardener to devote a large part of the garden to them.

Brassicas should be carefully rotated in the garden plan, with three to five years between each planting in the same bed. When preparing a bed for brassicas, apply lime at the rate of 6 pounds per 100 square feet. This provides the plant with adequate calcium to resist diseases, and raises the pH, making conditions less favorable to club-root.

All brassica beds should be double-dug and kept well cultivated. Double digging improves drainage and increases soil pore space, thereby minimizing high moisture content during the growing season. Amend the planting bed with adequate amounts of compost or composted manure, 1 to 2 inches deep. The organic matter also improves soil tilth, providing improved pore space in the soil.

All mustard family weeds should be kept to a minimum. Gardeners may miss shepherd's purse or shot weed as tasty winter salad additions, but this is a reasonable price to pay to avoid club-root.—CE

November

December

In the Garden

About this time every year the garden looks like it could use a little cleanup. Fall leaves have lost their color and are molding on the ground. Their blooms long since gone, flower stalks and stems rattle in the wind. The garden has, well—basically gone to seed.

Now most any gardening tome will tell you that garden hygiene and cleanliness are paramount in the control of pests and diseases. Up to a point this is true. Summer-growing tropical fruits and vegetables are susceptible to a whole host of fungal diseases that are easily transmitted and spread if their refuse is left randomly about the garden. So off goes the debris of tomatoes, peppers, cucumbers, squash, eggplant, potatoes and bush beans to a hot compost pile, not to be used on any summer crops next year.

Be ruthless with any other crops that show signs of disease, such as basal rot in garlic, club-root in brassicas or botrytis stem rot on any number of crops. These plants should be banished to the trash bin.

The tedious raking of leaves was mentioned last month, but tidy gardeners will frequently go to extremes when cleaning up (and cutting back) the garden. Tidy gardeners clip spent flowers and seed pods off the plants or cut down stalks of perennials past their prime. Setting seed is vital to plants' hardening off process for winter; if a gardener deadheads perennials too early, the plant does not go properly dormant. Besides, redheaded finches, chickadees and bush tits will nibble on seeds of fennel, globe thistle, bachelor buttons and others. On a cold winter morning with frost coating all the strange stalks and stems about the garden, be reminded that brown is a color too.—CE

December

Midwinter festivals honor the light, and in doing so encourage it to return. Evergreen trees and boughs traditionally represent rebirth and the circle of life.

Inviting Wildlife to the Harvest

A biologically diverse garden creates habitat for wild birds—beneficial creatures that will consume insects and provide delight the whole year round. Listed here are some parts that make up a healthy habitat, but a habitat is more than the sum of its parts. As your garden matures, interactions will unfold.

Provide water for birds and insects. Elaborate ponds with waterfalls and running water are unnecessary—shallow baths or bowls for bugs to sip from will do. Bug bowls are shallow containers filled with rocks and water. The rocks allow insects to land and sip water as it evaporates. Overhead watering creates drinking areas on leaves and makes small depressions or puddles that provide water for insects and birds.

All birds and insects need shelter. Build appropriate bird houses and leave a brush pile where birds can hide. A rotten log or stump can be a house for birds and insects, as well as being a landscape feature (and perhaps a radical horticultural statement). A favorite with children is a beetle house of rocks where ground beetles and spiders can find shelter for the winter.

Most people forget that birds need to feel safe and protected just like humans. Make sure your plantings provide layers of vegetation from the ground up to the tree canopy. Plants trimmed and shorn into tight geometric shapes do not provide adequate cover due to their interwoven stems, nor do plants standing in isolation. A good habitat aims to create corridors of contiguous foliage. Connect areas of your garden with a seamless tapestry of foliage where birds will feel welcome.

Food for thought: Birds will eat many pest insects, especially when laying eggs and when feeding their chicks. As a general rule, native plants in conjunction with a diverse habitat will do the best job of attracting native birds, though some introduced plants also work well.—CE

Shelter and Food Plants for Birds (a short list)

The individual plants listed are important, but more vital is providing a diverse habitat.

Herbaceous Plants

Angelica spp.
Asters *Aster* spp.
Borage *Borago officinalis*
Fennel *Foeniculum vulgare*
Globe Thistle *Echinops* spp.
Clover *Trifolium* spp.
Goldenrod *Solidago* spp.
Grasses (let go to seed)
Evergreen Ferns
Kale (let go to seed)
Parsley *Petroselinum* spp.
Phacelia spp.
Valerian *Valeriana* spp.
Vetch *Vicia* spp.

Shrubs

California Lilac *Ceanothus* spp.
Currents and Gooseberries *Ribes* spp.
Elderberry *Sambucus* spp.
Evergreen Huckleberry *Vaccinium ovatum*
Honeysuckle *Lonicera hispidula, L. ciliosa* and *L. involucrata*
Indian Plum *Osmaronia cerasiformis*
Kinnikinnik and Manzanita *Arctostaphylos* spp.
Ocean Spray *Holodiscus discolor*
Oregon Grape *Mahonia aquifolium, Mahonia nervosa*
Pacific Wax Myrtle *Myrica californica*
Red Twig Dogwood *Cornus stolonifera*
Salal *Gaultheria shallon*
Salmonberry *Rubus spectabilis*
Serviceberry *Amelanchier alnifolia*
Silk-Tassel *Garrya elliptica*
Shrub Roses *Rosa nutkana*
Thimbleberry *Rubus parviflorus*
Viburnum *Viburnum edule, Viburnum opulus*

Trees

Bitter Cherry *Prunus emarginata*
Black Hawthorn *Crataegus douglasii*
Cascara *Rhamnus purshiana*
Crab Apple *Malus* spp.
Chinquapin *Castanopsis chrysophylla*
Douglas Fir *Pseudotsuga menziesii*
Garry Oak *Quercus garryana*
Madrona *Arbutus menziesii*
Mountain Ash *Sorbus* spp.
Pine *Pinus* spp.
Strawberry Tree *Arbutus unedo*
Western Hemlock *Tsuga heterophylla*
Vine Maple *Acer circinatum*
Yew *Taxus brevifolia*

Planted Habitats Buzz With Rewards

A recent study shows great rewards reaped by farmers who created permanent strips of habitat for beneficial insects. Farmers sowed "habitat plantings" 1- meter wide the lengths of their fields. They used mat-forming perennial grasses and flowers and left the areas uncut for two years. Entomologists then sampled for insects. They found more than 100 times the populations of beneficials in the habitat strips than outside of them. These insects were also foraging 10 meters into the fields to dine on pest insects. This study's most important message is to leave an untidy mat of foliage near your vegetable garden where beneficial insects can overwinter.—CE

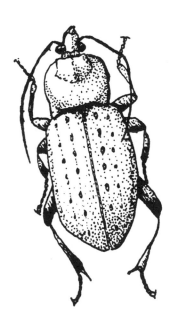

How Does Your Garden Grow?

One of the most helpful and least used garden tools is a good record book. It can be as simple or as complex as you like, but the rewards of recording the details of what happens in your garden have great benefits as the years progress.

Start by drawing the general shape of your garden and sketch in the garden beds; give each bed a number or a name. Put this garden map in a notebook and make a section for each bed separated by a tab. Every year, put in a new blank page for each bed, providing enough space to record up to three rotations. If you sow more than one crop at time in a bed, roughly sketch in where one crop ends and the other begins; this is especially useful if the planting area has an unusual shape.

In deciding what information is important to record, remember that with growing things, everything is important. But to begin with, for each bed write down when you sowed, what you planted, what soil amendments you used and note the weather conditions. As the plants grow (or don't), include any noteworthy things that happen. Do ladybugs like to visit? Are slugs taking over? Is there a disease problem? Are those your best peas ever? Mark down when and about how much you harvested—noting especially tasty varieties.

These records can be especially useful for planning rotations, and allow you more time to garden and less time for scratching your head and asking yourself, "Now what did I do that worked last year?"—KT

Resources

Where Gardeners Can Get Help

General Gardening Questions

Master Gardeners

Sponsored by the state university Cooperative Extension, Master Gardeners are trained to answer plant-related questions. To find a Master Gardener in your area, look in the government listings in your phone book under County Government for Cooperative Extension. Often Master Gardeners have their own question telephone line. Be sure to ask for organic solutions.

Seattle Tilth

4649 Sunnyside Ave. N., Rm. 1; Seattle, WA 98103;
(206) 633-0451; fax (206) 633-0450;
email: gardenstaff@seattletilth.org   website: www.seattletilth.org

Vashon Island Growers Association (VIGA)

P.O. Box 2894; Vashon, WA 98070; (206) 567-4026

Spokane Tilth

4629 N. Hartley St., Spokane, WA 99205; (509) 326-5466

South Whidbey Tilth

P.O. Box 252; Langley, WA 98260; (360) 221-2998

Permaculture Implementation Guild of Seattle

P.O. Box 45472; Seattle, WA 98145

Oregon Tilth

1860 Hawthorne Ave. NE, Suite 200; Salem, OR 97303
(503) 998-3069; fax (503) 998-1192; email: organic@tilth.org
website: www.tilth.org

Oregon Tilth is an organic agriculture organization advocating for and providing education about practices which create and support a healthful sustainable food supply. Oregon Tilth continues to provide leadership and direction in the certification of organic food products regionally and internationally. Oregon Tilth has five local chapters:

> **Yamhill**
> Contact: Derek & Sharon Goad at (541) 852-6141. Meetings the 4th Tuesday of the month.
>
> **Southern Willamette Valley**
> Contact Kayleen Hanna at (541) 343-5201.
>
> **Portland**
> Contact: Liz Marantz at (503) 246-7185. Meetings the 2nd Monday of the month. The Portland chapter sponsors a garden tour each year, usually in August.
>
> **Siskiyou**
> Contact: The Oregon Tilth office at (503) 998-3069. Meetings

the 2nd Sunday of the month. In January this chapter holds a winter seed exchange. They also sponsor spring and fall symposiums, and series of courses in organic gardening held from February though April.

> **Corvallis**
> Contact: Linda Kapuler (541) 752-0421. Meetings the 2nd Sunday of the month. The Corvallis chapter hosts a spring fertilizer sale.

Questions About Trees

PlantAmnesty

P.O. Box 15377; Seattle, WA 98115-0377; (206) 783-9813;
email: plantamnes@aol.com website: www.plantamnesty.org

Arboretum Foundation

2300 Arboretum Drive E.; Seattle, WA 98112-2300;
(206) 325-4510

Friends of the Trees

P.O. Box 4469, Bellingham, WA 98227; (360) 738-4972;
website: www.geocities.com/RainForest

TREEmendous Seattle

7400 Sand Point Way NE; Seattle, WA 98115; (206) 985-6867

Questions About Compost

City Farmer Regional Compost Hotline at Canada's Office of Urban Agriculture

#801-318 Homer St.; Vancouver, BC V6B 2V3 CANADA
(604) 736-2250; fax (604) 685-0431; email:
cityfarm@interchange.ubc.ca website: www.cityfarmer.org

Seattle Compost Hotline

4649 Sunnyside Ave. N., Rm. 1; Seattle, WA 98103;
(206) 633-0224; FAX (206) 633-0450; email:
compost@seattletilth.org

Metro (Portland, OR) Recycling Information Hotline

(503) 234-3000; email: mri@metro.dst.or.us

Master Recycler/Composter Program

OSU Extension-Energy Program, 800 NE Oregon, Suite 450, Portland, OR 97323-2140; (503) 731-4104

Also contact the Solid Waste or Public Utility in your area for Master Recycler/Composter Programs sponsored though your county Cooperative Extension.

Questions About Toxic Substances and Pesticides

Washington Toxics Coalition
4649 Sunnyside Ave. N; Suite 540 East; Seattle, WA 98103;
(206) 632-1545; fax (206) 632-8661; email: info@watoxics.org
website: www.watoxics.org

Northwest Coalition for Alternatives to Pesticides
P.O. Box 1393, Eugene, OR 97440-1393; (541) 344-5044
email: info@pesticide.org   website: www.pesticide.org

Bulk Compost in Washington and Oregon

WASHINGTON

Whatcom County
Finkbonner & Sons (360) 384-3232

Mushroom Compost
DeWilde Nursery (360) 733-8190
Bakerview Nursery (360) 676-0400 or 380-9097

Island County
Coopeville Transfer Station (360) 679-7386

King County
Cedar Grove Compost (425) 432-2395
  Available in bulk throughout King, Pierce, and Snohomish
  counties. Look under "topsoil" in the phone book.
Pacific Topsoils (800) 884-7645 or (425) 486-3201
Sawdust Supply Company (206) 622-4321
Sayers Fuel (206) 723-4255

Kitsap County
Land Recovery, Inc. (253) 884-3622
Purdy Topsoil (253) 857-5850
Vern's Organic Topsoil & Bark (360) 779-2764
Stewart's Topsoil for Less (360) 479-7645 or (360) 697-4255

Pierce County
Land Recovery, Inc. (253) 581-9594

Mushroom Compost
H & B Fuel & Topsoil (253) 472-1252

Thurston County
Hawk's Prairie Landfill Compost Center (360) 459-7347

Mushroom Compost
Great Western Supply Company (360) 754-3722

Clark County
H & H Wood Recyclers (360) 892-2805
McFarlane's Bark (360) 892-6125

Composted Manures
DeJongs (Chicken & Chips Product) (206) 885-1821
Smith Brothers Dairy (cow manure) (253) 682-7633
Mystic Lake Goat Dairy (goat manure) (425) 868-2029
Zoo Doo (herbivore manure) (206) 625-7667

OREGON

Washington and Multnomah Counties
Allwood Recyclers (503) 667-5497
American Compost and Recycling, Inc. (503) 286-0886
Bark Blowers, Inc. (503) 648-2275
Best Buy in Town (503) 645-6665
DeVoe Landscaping (503) 684-6169
Grimm's Fuel Co. (503) 692-3756
McFarlane's Bark (503) 659-4240
Minsinger Floral Nursery (503) 636-1843
River Cities One-Stop Recycling Center (503) 655-1928
S & H Logging (503) 638-1011
Oregon Bark (503) 682-3301
Clackamas Compost Products (503) 557-1028
Lakeside Reclamation/Grobhorn, Inc. (503) 628-1866

Leaf Compost
City of Portland Leaf Compost (503) 287-5142

Marion County
Wood Waste Reclamation (503) 371-6291

Mushroom Compost
Yarnell Bark and Nursery (503) 581-0441
Picsweet Mushroom Farm (503) 581-2471

Benton County
Processing Recover Center (541) 745-5831

Lane County
Rexius (800) 652-7368
Lane Forest Products (541) 345-9085

For Manure Products

Many conservation districts sponsor horse manure share programs.
Many cow or goat dairies also sell manures. Check availability in
your local area.

Worm Castings (Vermicompost)

Worms and worm bins are available through Seattle Tilth. See page 44
for details on making your own vermicompost. It can be purchased
commercially from the Yelm Earth Worm Farm, (360) 894-0707.

Websites on Gardening in the Pacific Northwest

www.seattletilth.org Information about Seattle Tilth events, workshops,
CSA listings, the Tilth store and the Children's Garden. You will also find
gardening tips, directions for building compost and worm bins, and forms
to become a member of Seattle Tilth or buy a Garden Guide for your friend!
www.nwgarden.com Forums, seed exchanges, pictures, and more from
fellow NW gardeners.
www.slugsandsalal.com This site is devoted exclusively to the Pacific
Coast region (from Prince Rupert on the central British Columbia coast
down through into northern California).
www.rainyside.com Two rainyside gardeners from Western Washington
teamed up for this site on Maritime NW gardening.
www.gardening.wsu.edu Website for the Washington State University Extension
www.wnps.org The Washington Native Plant Society
www.eesc.orst.edu Website for Oregon State University Extension Program
www.tammyslug.com The Official Pacific Northwest Slug Page

Reference Books and Materials

Look for out-of-print books at used bookstores, or try a used book search through www.powells.com or www.amazon.com

General Gardening Books

Encyclopedia of Organic Gardening (Rodale Press, 2000) A good general reference book on organic gardening; however, most of the specific recommendations are more appropriate to the East Coast and Midwest.

The New Sunset Western Garden Book by the editors of Sunset Books (6th edition, Sunset Publishing Co., 1997) Convenient encyclopedia, useful for its brief descriptions of cultural information and propagation, and zone maps. A standard reference for western gardeners.

The Northwest Gardeners' Resource Directory by Stephanie Feeney (Cedarcroft Press, yearly updates) An accessible resource for nurseries, plant sales, and practically anything a Maritime Northwest gardener needs.

The Year in Bloom By Ann Lovejoy (Sasquatch Books, 1989) the first of many of Ann Lovejoy's insightful and inspiring books on ornamental horticulture for our region.

Gardening For The Future Of The Earth by Howard-Yana Shapiro and John Harrisson (Bantam, 2000) Writings on the philosophy of sustainable gardening along with helpful tips on organic growing.

Vegetable Gardening

Creative Vegetable Gardening by Joy Larkcom (2nd edition, Artabras Press, 1999)

Oriental Vegetables by Joy Larkcom (2nd edition, Kodansha International, 1994)

The Salad Garden by Joy Larkcom (2nd edition, Penguin USA, 1996) These three books above provide well-organized introductions to superior vegetable varieties and the cultural advice is thoughtful and clearly written. This quality of authorship is rarely found in U.S. gardening books.

The Vegetable Garden by M.M. Vilmorin-Andrieux (OUT OF PRINT, most recent edition was Ten Speed Press,1981) First published in 1885, this is an incredible resource for cultural techniques and to get an idea about the state of market gardening before the modern age. Beautiful etchings accompany most vegetable descriptions.

Growing Vegetables West of the Cascades by Steve Solomon (5th edition, Sasquatch Books, 2000) Practical information that all Maritime Northwest gardeners will find indispensible. Written by the founder of the Territorial Seed Company.

Winter Gardening in the Maritime Northwest by Binda Colebrook (3rd edition, Sasquatch Books, 1998) A charming read throughout, it will inspire and provide information to awaken the winter gardener within.

How to Grow More Vegetables by John Jeavons (5th edition, Ten Speed Press, 1995) A solid general resource providing information about how to cultivate vegetables with the bio-intensive raised bed technique.

Designing and Maintaining Your Edible Landscape—Naturally by Robert Kourik (OUT OF PRINT, most recent edition was Metamorphic Press, 1986) A full-service reference for the city dweller or small landholder, everything from soil improvement to fruits.

Growing Great Garlic by Ron L. Engeland (Filaree Productions, 1995) The garlic grower's dream, a heartfelt and methodical examination of everything a gardener or farmer needs to grow garlic.

The Food Lover's Garden by Angelo M. Pellegrini (The Lyons Press, 1999) Pour a glass of wine, make some crostini, and experience any enjoyable read full of wonderful advice from someone you may wish was your grandfather.

Gardening Under Cover by William Head (Sasquatch Books, 1989) Great explanation of microclimates and about how to use season extenders to your best advantage in the Maritime Northwest.

Cornucopia: A Source Book of Edible Plants by Stephen Facciola (Kampong Publications, 1990) A listing and description of more than 10,000 edible, medicinal, and useful plants from around the world. A must for any plant fanatic.

The New Organic Grower by Eliot Coleman (2nd revised edition, Chelsea Green Publishing, 1995) Clearly explains some of the more esoteric cultural techniques of organic growing. A down-to-earth kind of reference book.

Culinary Herbs

Book of Herbs by Roger Phillips and Nicky Foy (Random House, 1990) One of a number of reasonably priced reference books from this publisher. A wide-ranging list of herbs are described including an outline for their cultural care. Full of good information—not fluff like a lot of herb books.

Growing Herbs for the Maritime Northwest Gardener by Mary Preus (Sasquatch Books, 1996) A great introduction to the cultivation of most common culinary herbs. The month-by-month calendar of herb garden tasks is very helpful.

Fruit Gardening, Pruning, and Trees

Pruning and Training by Christopher Brickell and David Joyce (American Horticulture Society, 1996) Quality illustrations about pruning. This is a very comprehensive book.

The Fruit Garden Displayed by Harry Baker (OUT OF PRINT, last edition The Royal Horticulture Society, 1951) Great pruning illustrations, but unfortunately, descriptions are of varieties not found in the U.S.

North American Landscape Trees by Arthur Lee Jacobsen (OUT OF PRINT, last edition Ten Speed Press, 1995) A comprehensive history and listing of trees in North America by Seattle Tilth's own Arthur Lee.

Complete Guide to Landscape Design, Renovation, and Maintenance by Cass Turnbull (F & W Publications, 1991) Got a jungle of a yard? This book has answers to many of the questions facing a backyard gardener.

Drip Irrigation

Drip Irrigation by Robert Kourik (Metamorphic Press, 1993) Written by someone who understands the cruel reality of installing plumbing. Most everything you need to know to install and maintain a drip irrigation system.

Insects and Plant Diseases

Rodale's Successful Organic Gardening: Controlling Pests and Diseases by Patricia S. Michalak (Rodale Press, 1994) A fine explanation of organic pest and disease control, with photos that make identification easy. Reasonable priced and easily found at most nurseries.

The Gardeners Guide to Common Sense Pest Control by William Olkowski, Sheila Daar, Helga Olkowski (The Taunton Press, 1996) Written by three pioneers of integrated pest management. Good information on insect monitoring, knowing when a pest can become a problem, and how to reduce pest damage with the least toxic methods.

Pests of the Garden and Small Farm by Mary Louise Flint (University of California, 1999) Written for California, but it provides practical identification, monitoring, and control techniques.

Attracting Birds and other Wildlife

The Bird Garden by Stephen W. Kress (Houghton Mifflin, 1995) Written by an authority on birds in North America, and packed with good information.

Naturescaping: A Place for Wildlife (Oregon Department of Fish and Wildlife) A superb book to assist urban gardeners in creating wildlife habitats appropriate to the Maritime Northwest. To order, call 503-872-5264, ext. 5528. As of this printing, they did not have the book available; however, a revised version is due out by the end of 2000.

The Butterfly Garden by Jerry Sedenko (OUT OF PRINT, last edition Villard Books,1991) The best book on the subject; good plant descriptions and through coverage of butterfly species across the U.S.

Composting and Soil Fertility

The Rodale Book of Composting edited by Deborah L. Martin and Grace Gershuny (Rodale Press, 1992) The Rodale organization re-introduced composting to the modern U.S. gardener, and their publications are still the best resource for the proper making and use of compost.

Start with the Soil by Grace Gershuny (Rodale Press, 1997) An entertaining and accurate book about soil in an organic garden. A must for beginning gardeners to understand the beautiful world down under.

Master Composter Training Manual edited by Howard Stenn (Seattle Solid Waste Utility, 1997) A must-have book for a compost-based community organizer. To order, contact the Compost Hotline at 206-633-0224.

Organic Guide to Compost and Mulch Gardening (OUT OF PRINT, last edition was Rodale Press, 1960) Compiled by the editorial staff of Organic Gardening and Farming published by Rodale Press. An old, small yet comprehensive guide.

Let it Rot by Stu Campbell (3rd edition, Storey Books 1998) Accessible, affordable guide to rot.

Worms Eat My Garbage by Mary Appelhof (Flower Press, 1997) The definitive work on worm bin composting.

Gardening with Children

Teaching Peace Through Gardening by Anne Pedersen (Seattle Tilth, 1996) A curriculum that helps children use experiences in the garden to support positive, peaceful approaches to problems and situations that occur among people outside the garden.

Worms Eat Our Garbage: Classroom Activities for a Better Environment by Mary Appelhof (Flower Press, 1993) Worksheets and activities for math, science, writing, and art—great resource for elementary school teachers.

The Worm Café: Mid-scale Vermicomposting of Lunchroom Wastes by Binet Payne (Flower Press, 1999) Everything you need to know about using worms to compost small scale amounts of lunchroom wastes.

Buffalo Bird Woman's Garden by Gilbert L. Wilson (Minnesota Historical Society Press, 1987) Focuses on a Native American approach to agriculture, good for children 11 and older. Available from the Minnesota Historical Society at 800-647-7827.

Organic Fertilizer Sources

These ingredients are useful for making custom blends to fit the needs of specific crop plants or to address soil needs after a soil test.

Nitrogen Sources

Nitrogen is important for plants to form proteins and grow new leaves. Many leafy greens, garlic and leeks benefit from a side dressing of organic nitrogen during their most active growth periods. This can be applied two or three times during the growing season.

Alfalfa Meal—5-0-2.5—Ground alfalfa hay in pellets. Some soluble nitrogen; provides a highly valuable slow-release source of nitrogen that will give benefits over a growing season.

Bat Guano—10-3-1—(8 percent calcium) Mined from old deposits of bat manure in caves, this is expensive but useful in small amounts as a top dressing.

Blood Meal—14-0-0—A by-product of slaughter houses. Very high in water-soluble nitrogen, useful for top dressing leaf crops and other heavy feeders in cold weather.

Cottonseed Meal—6-.5-1.5—Used as a nutrient source for growing plants that prefer an acid soil, such as blueberries or certain ornamentals. Cotton production is heavily dependent on pesticides, and very few suppliers of cottonseed meal test for pesticide residues or make any claims about its purity.

Feather Meal—11-3-0—Steamed and pulverized poultry feathers, this meal is great to add to compost high in carbon. This is a common addition to commercially blended organic fertilizers due to its light weight.

Fish Meal—10-6-2 and trace minerals—A by-product of fish processing, this meal is a fine source of slow-release nutrients, and works very well for summer crops.

Shrimp Shell Meal—5-8-0—(15 percent calcium, 18 percent chitin) Ground shrimp shells very slowly release nutrients. This meal is recommended for the control of nematodes and symphylan.

Microbes and fungi increase to breakdown the chitin in shrimp shells, then the organisms consume the chitin-based exo-skeleton of nematodes and symphylans, thereby reducing these soil pests.

Phosphorus

The main function of phosphorus is to act as a catalyst in releasing carbohydrate energy in the plant and to transfer energy from one point to another. Phosphorus promotes the growth of fine root hairs, brings vitality to blooms and fruit, and is concentrated in seeds to assist in the germination process.

Bone Meal—1-11-0—(20 percent calcium) A by-product of slaughter houses, bone meal has high amounts of water-soluble phosphorus. This is useful as an amendment in the early years of a garden and for crops needing great amounts of phosphorus.

Fish Bone Meal—2-8-0—A replacement for domestic mammal bone meal.

Colloidal (Soft) Rock Phosphate—0-16-0—(19 percent calcium) The best source for long-term availability of phosphorus and calcium, as the nutrients are available to crops for up to five years.

Potassium and Trace Minerals

Potassium is vital for carbohydrate metabolism and the growth of new cells. It assists in the absorption of nitrogen, calcium and trace minerals. Trace minerals are needed in small amounts to act as a catalyst for plant metabolism, vitamin formation, nitrogen processes and chlorophyll synthesis.

Azomite—0-0-2.5 and trace minerals—Popularized in the book *Secrets of the Soil* as "Glacial Rock Dust," Azomite is a marine clay deposit that is high in potash and trace minerals.

Greensand (glauconite)—0-0-7 and trace minerals—Mined from 70-million-year-old deposits, greensand contains slow-release potassium to build up soil reserves.

Granite Dust—0-0-4 and trace minerals—A by-product of quarries and stoneworkers, granite dust is an inexpensive and useful amendment to slowly build potassium reserves. One application can last up to eight years in the soil.

Kelp Meal—1.5-0.5-2.5 and trace minerals—Dried and ground kelp is harvested from both the Atlantic and Pacific oceans. Kelp meal stimulates soil biological activity and works well to quickly adjust potassium deficiencies.

Sunflower Seed Hulls—0-0-11—When ground to a dust, sunflower seed hulls are a good, lightweight source of potassium. The nutrient will not be available under cold or low organic matter conditions.

Wood Ashes—0-0-7 and trace minerals—Ashes are very water-soluble and quickly leach from the root zones of plants. Be sure to use only natural wood, no lumber or treated lumber.

Fertilizer Sources

Peaceful Valley Farm Supply (919) 272-4769

Planet Natural (406) 587-5891

Integrated Fertility Management (800) 332-3179

Walt's Organic Fertilizer Co. (206) 783-6685

How to Calculate How Much of Each Nutrient is Needed from Soil Test Results

Soil tests sent to a laboratory often come back with results and recommendations more appropriate to a farm than to a garden. The recommendations for a specific nutrient are usually in pounds of actual nutrient needed per acre to grow good vegetables. To figure out how much nutrient is needed to add to a garden, two series of math calculations need to be done.

1. Converting pounds per acre to pounds per 100 square feet.

    For example, a soil test recommends to add 100 pounds of nitrogen per acre to grow a garden. This garden occupies 100 square feet of space. Divide 100 by 435, the approximate number of 100 square foot units in an acre:

    $$100 \div 435 = .23$$

    .22 lb. of nitrogen needs to be added to a 100-square-foot garden

2. Figure the amount of organic soil amendment to add to supply the nutrient.

    For example, alfalfa meal contains 5 percent available nitrogen (5-0-2.5). Divide the number of pounds of nutrient needed by the percent of the nutrient in the soil amendment:

    $$.23 \div .05 = 4.6$$

    In this example, 4.6 pounds of alfalfa meal will need to be added to a 100-square-foot garden to supply the necessary nitrogen. (Q.E.D.— and you thought you would never use your math skills again.)

Coverage of Bulk Material (compost, manure, etc.)

1 cubic foot covers:	1 cubic yard covers:
24 square feet ½ inch deep	648 square feet ½ inch deep
12 square feet 1 inch deep	324 square feet 1 inch deep
6 square feet 2 inches deep	162 square feet 2 inches deep
4 square feet 3 inches deep	108 square feet 3 inches deep

Dilution Chart for Organic Liquid Fertilizers and Teas

DILUTION OF TEA	AMOUNT OF WATER		
	1 quart	1 gallon	3 gallons
1-3	11 ounces	42 ounces	1 gallon
1-4	8 ounces	2 pints	3 quarts
1-5	6 ounces	25 ounces	2 quarts + 12 ounces
1-10	3 ounces	12 ounces	12 ounces

Herb and Vegetable Planting Guidelines

Herbs	Harvest Season	Space Between Plants	Seed Life (yrs)	Cool/Warm Season	Annual/ Biennial/Perennial
Anis Hyssop (*Agastache*)	June-Aug	8"	3	C	P
Basil (*Ocimum basilicum*)	July-Aug	12"	4	W	A
Borage (*Borago*)	June-July	15"	3	C/W	A
Caraway (*Carum carvi*)	Spring	6"	3	C/W	B
Chervil (*Anthriscus*)	May-July	4"	5	C	A
Chives (*Alium schoenoprasum*)	Mar-June	6-12"	2	C	P
Cilantro (*Coriandrum*)	Spring	4-6"	4	C	A
Dill (*Anethum*)	July-Sept	6-8"	2	W	A
Fennel (*Foeniculum*)	July-Oct	12"	3	C/W	P
Fenugreek (*Trigonella*)	July	6"	5	W	A
Garlic (*Allium sativum*)	Summer	3"	1	C	P
Garlic Chives	Mar-June	6-12"	3	C	P
Lavender (*Lavendula*)	June-July	24"	2	W	P
Lemon Balm (*Melissa*)	June-Sept	18-24"	4	C/W	P
Lovage (*Levisticum officinale*)	June-July	36"	3	C/W	P
Marjoram (*Origanum majorana*)	Aug-/Sept	12"	4	C/W	P
Oregano (*O. heracleoticum*)	July-Sept	18-24"	4	C/W	P
Parsley (*Petroselinum*)	Spring/Fall	4"	3	C	B
Peppermint (*Mentha piperita*)	July-Aug	12"	2	C	P
Perilla	Summer	10"	2	W	A
Sage (*Salvia officinalis*)	June	12-18"	5	C/W	P
Salad Burnet (*Poterium*)	May-June	6"	4	C	P
Summer Savory (*Satureja hortensis*)	July	6"	4	W	A
Sorrel (*Rumex acetosa*)	Spring/Fall	12"	3	C	P
Spearmint	July-Aug	15"	3	C/W	P
Tarragon (*Artemisia dracunculus*)	July-Aug	18"	–	W	P
Thyme (*Thymus vulgaris*)	All Year	6"	4	C/W	P
Yarrow (*Achillea*)	June-Sept	6"	4	W	P

Vegetables, continued	Length to Harvest in Days	Space Between Plants	Seed Life (yrs)	Cool/Warm Season	Annual/ Biennial/Perennial
Amaranth Greens	30-45	8"	3	W	A
Artichoke	1-2 yrs	24-36"	–	W	P
Asparagus (Root Crowns)	2-3 yrs	18"	–	C	P
Beans, Bush	60-80	4-6"	3	W	A
Beans, Pole	70-90	6-8"	3	W	A
Beets	50-80	2-5"	5	C	B

Vegetables, continued	Harvest Season	Space Between Plants	Seed Life (yrs)	Cool/Warm Season	Annual/ Biennial/Perennial
Broccoli (Spring)	60-90	18-24"	4	C	B
Broccoli (Winter)	220-250	18-24"	4	C	B
Brussels Sprouts	100-180	18-24"	4	C	B
Cabbage (Spring)	60-80	18-24"	4	C	B
Cabbage (Winter)	75-210	18-24"	4	C	B
Cabbage, Chinese	60-80	10-18"	4	C	B
Cardoon	120	24-36"	4	C	P
Carrot	65-90	1-2"	3	C	B
Cauliflower (Spring)	60-85	18-24"	5	C	A
Cauliflower (Winter)	220-260	18-24"	5	C	A
Celeriac	110-120	10"	5	C	B
Celery	115-130	6-12"	5	C	B
Chard, Swiss	50-60	18-24"	5	W	B
Chicory/Radicchio	60-100	4-8"	3	C	A
Collards	40-90	12"	3	C	B
Corn	65-105	8-16"	2	W	A
Corn Salad	60-80	3"	3	C	A
Cress	10-30	2"	5	C	A
Cucumber	60-80	12-18"	7	W	A
Eggplant	70-80	18-24"	5	W	A
Endive/Escarole	60-85	12"	5	W	A
Fava Beans	180	6-8"	3	C	A
Good King Henry	60	12"	1	C	P
Jerusalem Artichokes	120	12"	1	C	P
Kale	45-65	12-18"	4	C	B
Kohlrabi	60	3-6"	4	C	B
Lamb's Quarters	30	3-6"	4	C	B
Leeks	80-150	3-4"	3	C	B
Letttuce	45-90	6-12"	5	C	A
Melons	90-120	16"	7	W	A
Miner's Lettuce	30-60	5-6"	2	C	A
Mustard	30-60	6-8"	4	C	A
Onions	100-120	1-3"	2	C	B
Orach	40-50	6-8"	2	W	A
Parsnips	100-120	3"	2	C	B
Peas	95-120	2-4"	3	C	A
Peppers	60-90	12-18"	4	W	A
Potatoes (Tubers)	80-140	10"	—	C	A
Pumpkin	100-115	24-30"	7	W	A
Purslane	45-60	4-6"	5	W	A

Vegetables, continued	Length to Harvest in Days	Space Between Plants	Seed Life (yrs)	Cool/Warm Season	Annual/ Biennial/Perennial
Rhubarb	1-2 yrs	3'	–	C	P
Rocket/Arugula	30-45	4-6"	4	C	A
Rutabaga	95	6-8"	5	C	B
Salsify	120	2"	2	C	B
Scorzonera	120	2"	2	C	B
Shungiku	60	6"	3	C	A
Spinach	40-50	3-4"	5	C	A
Spinach, New Zealand	80	8-12"	3	C	A
Squash (Summer)	50-70	18-24"	5	W	A
Squash (Winter)	90-120	18-24"	5	W	A
Tomatoes	70-90	18-24"	4	W	A
Turnip	30-55	2-4"	5	C	A

Organic Gardening Glossary

Aerobic: An environment containing oxygen.

Aggregate: A group of soil particles that hold together, these are the building blocks of soil structure.

Anaerobic: An environment without oxygen.

Beneficial Insect: An insect that benefits plants by eating or parasitizing pest insects or by pollinating flowers.

Biodiversity: A healthy environment known for the presence of myriad and diverse living and dead organisms.

Bolt: The process of a plant going prematurely to seed.

Castings: Earthworm excrement.

Biomass: The total weight of plant material growing in a given area.

Compaction: The pressing together and pressing down of soil particles by foot or other traffic.

Compost: To compost is to use any of several methods to speed up the decomposition of raw organic matter, usually by aerating and moistening piles of materials containing carbon and nitrogen. Compost is the result of these efforts, a crumbly, nutrient-rich natural fertilizer.

Cotylelon: First leaves of a plant, sometimes called seed leaves. They look immature and chubby.

Cover crop: A crop that improves and protects the soil in which it is grown.

Cultural Techniques: Gardening techniques to care and tend for plants.

Damping Off: A fungal disease of young seedlings, causing the stem to rot.

Decomposers: Soil bacteria and other larger organisms that are nourished by breaking down the remains or wastes of other organisms into simple organic compounds.

Determinate, Tomato: Sets flowers and fruits over a short period and tends to ripen all at once; short, bushy plants.

Evaporation: The loss of water from the surface of the soil.

Fertilizer: Any material added to the soil to provide essential nutrients to plants.

Foliar fertilizer: Liquid fertilizer applied directly to plant leaves,
usually as a fine spray over the leaf surface.

Frost Dates (first and last): The first and last day an area experiences freezing temperatures.

Green Manure: A cover crop used to protect the soil, hold or build nutrients and smother weeds.

Harden Off: To slowly introduce a seedling or transplant that has been growing indoors or with the protection of a cloche or other shelter into the outdoor garden.

Heat Units (HU): The number of hours the air temperature remains above 65° F. The Puget Sound receives 1500 HU in an average summer. The Willamette Valley receives approximately 1800 HU.

Herbaceous: Plant matter that is soft and green; plants that do not form woody tissue.

Humus: The result of organic matter binding with minerals in the soil to create a moist, deep-brown, rich healthy tilth.

Hybrid: A plant that is a genetic dead-end, meaning the seeds from a hybrid plant will not give rise to the exact same or very similar plant.

Indeterminate, Tomato: Vines continue to flower and fruit throughout the season; tall plants.

Inoculant: Spores of a desired strain of Rhizobium bacteria applied in powder form to the appropriate legume seed for planting. Also, any material of high microbial content added to soil or compost to stimulate biological activity.

Leaching: The movement (usually loss) of dissolved nutrients as water percolates through the soil.

Legume: A member of the plant family *Leguminosae* (including clover, alfalfa, beans and peas), which roots host nitrogen-fixing bacteria in a symbiotic relationship.

Ley Crop: A crop set aside to improve the soil for two or more years; frequently cut to make compost.

Macronutrient: A plant nutrient needed in substantial quantities, including carbon, hydrogen, silica, oxygen, nitrogen, phosphorus, sulfur, calcium, magnesium and potassium.

Metabolism: The biochemical processes of growth, maintenance and energy transformation necessary for a living organism.

Micronutrient: A plant nutrient needed in very small quantities, including copper, chlorine, zinc, iron, manganese, boron and molybdenum.

Mineralization: The release of water-soluble mineral and simple organic compounds through the decomposition of organic matter.

Nitrogen Fixation: The conversion of gaseous nitrogen into complex chemical compounds that can eventually be used by a plant.

Nursery Bed: A protected area in the garden where seedlings are nurtured.

Open-Pollinated: Unlike hybrids, plants that will return in the same form from their seed.

Organic Matter: The living part of the soil comprised of decomposing plant and animal materials, and huge amounts of microorganisms.

Overwinter: Any plant that is either planted out or sown in the late summer to grow throughout the fall and winter months for harvest in spring.

Parasitoid: An insect which uses another insect as a nursery for its eggs.

Petiole: The stalk of a leaf.

Pricking Out: The process of gently transplanting seedlings from a flat into larger pots.

Pulses: Legume seeds for human consumption: beans, peas, favas, lentils, etc.

Rhizobia: A group of bacteria that penetrates the roots of legumes, extracts carbohydrates from the plant and fixes gaseous nitrogen in the soil which plants can use.

Sclerotia: The fruiting bodies of some fungi.

Soil Amendment: Any material added to the soil to promote biological activity.

Soil pH: The pH of the water in the soil, which controls the availability of phosphorous and trace elements, and the diversity of soil organisms. The soil pH for most soils ranges from 5.0 to 9.0, with 7.0 being neutral.

Soil Structure: The density and size of soil aggregates. A good soil. structure is comprised of aggregates of widely varying size.

Soil: An ecological system consisting of inorganic minerals, organic matter and living organisms.

Sub-Tropical or Tender Plants: Plants that cannot survive even a light amount of frost, which require adequate heat to grow well.

Symbiotic: The mutually beneficial interrelationship between two organisms, such as nitrogen-fixing rhizobia and the roots of legume plants.

Tilth: An English word used to describe the structure and quality of soil, similar to the concept of health. In the medieval monastic tradition the word was used to describe the cultivation of wisdom and spirit.

Top Dressing: Compost or fertilizer applied to a growing crop, usually worked into the top 1-2 inches of topsoil.

Transpiration: Water loss through leaves.

True Leaves: The leaves of a plant that grow after the cotyledons.

Undersow: To sow seeds underneath an existing growing crop without digging the soil.

Variety: A cultivated, named form of a plant species demonstrating unique characteristics.

Vegan: A vegetarian whose diet consists of plants and plant products only.

Date _____   ☐ New   ☐ Renewal

Name(s)/Organizaton _____

Address _____

City/State/Zip _____ Is this a new address? _____

Home/Message Phone _____ Neighborhood _____

Email Address: _____

Membership dues: ☐ $25 Regular   ☐ $50 Supporting   ☐ $100 Sustaining
                    ☐ $500 Lifetime   ☐ $15 Low Income

Tax-deductible contribution to the Seattle Tilth Association $ _____

I'm interested in working on the following program(s):

☐ Fundraising   ☐ Membership   ☐ Education   ☐ Garden   ☐ Newsletter   ☐ Children's Garden   ☐ Library
☐ Plant Sale   ☐ Harvest Fair   ☐ Office Support   ☐ Farm Programs   ☐ Compost Classes   ☐ Organic Wine Tasting

Membership Form

Mail to: Seattle Tilth Association
            4649 Sunnyside Ave. N., Rm. 1
            Seattle, WA 98103
            ATTN: Membership   Or Call: (206) 633-0451

Notes

Notes